PROJECT
SUCCESS

INTRO

Sarah Lynn

Series Consultants
Susan Gaer
Sarah Lynn

The publisher would like to thank Irene Frankel for her creative conception and vision for this groundbreaking course.

PROJECT SUCCESS INTRO

Pearson Education, 10 Bank Street, White Plains, NY 10606

Staff Credits: The people who made up the *Project Success* team, representing editorial, production, design, and manufacturing, are Peter Benson, Andrea Bryant, Maretta Callahan, Iris Candelaria, Aerin Csigay, Mindy DePalma, Dave Dickey, Christine Edmonds, Nancy Flaggman, Ann France, Aliza Greenblatt, Gosia Jaros-White, Caroline Kasterine, Amy Kefauver, Niki Lee, Jaime Lieber, Jessica Miller-Smith, Tracey Munz Cataldo, Laurie Neaman, Jenn Raspiller, Julie Schmidt, Kim Snyder, Katherine Sullivan, Loretta Steeves, Jane Townsend, Ken Volcjak, and Martin Yu.

Interior Design: Word & Image

Cover Design: Ann France and Tracey Munz Cataldo

Text Composition: TSI Graphics

Text font: Franklin Gothic

For photo and illustration credits, please turn to the back of the book.

Library of Congress Cataloging-in-Publication Data
Lynn, Sarah.
  Project success : skills for the 21st century / Sarah Lynn ; Series Consultants: Susan Gaer, Sarah Lynn.
      pages cm
  Summary: Project Success is a blended-learning digital and print course with a strong focus on workplace skills, career readiness, and 21st century challenges. This unique video-based series engages learners with high-interest video vignettes that represent a "day in the life" of characters in diverse workplace settings that may simulate their own. Integrated skills lessons encourage critical thinking and problem solving woven into the students' English language learning journey.
    ISBN 978-0-13-294236-2 — ISBN 978-0-13-248297-4 — ISBN 978-0-13-294238-6 — ISBN 978-0-13-294240-9 — ISBN 978-0-13-294242-3 — ISBN 978-0-13-298513-0
  1. English language—Textbooks for foreign speakers. 2. English language—Spoken English. 3. English language—Sound recordings for foreign speakers. 4. English language—Study and teaching—Foreign speakers—Audio-visual aids. 5. Business communication—United States—Vocational guidance. I. Gaer, Susan. II. Title.
    PE1128.L98 2014
    428.2'4—dc23
                                                              2013035851

ISBN-10:   0-13-294236-4
ISBN-13: 978-0-13-294236-2

Printed in the United States of America
3   17

Contents

Acknowledgments

The authors and publisher would like to offer sincere thanks to our Series Consultants for lending their expertise and insights and for helping shape the course.

Susan Gaer Santa Ana College School of Continuing Education, Santa Ana, CA

Sarah Lynn Harvard Bridge to Learning and Literacy Program, Cambridge, MA

In addition, we would like to express gratitude to the following people. Their kind participation was invaluable to the creation of this program.

Consultants

Robert Breitbard, Director of Adult & Community Education, Collier County Public Schools, Naples, Florida; **Ingrid Greenberg**, Associate Professor, ESL, and Past-President, Academic Senate, Continuing Education, San Diego Community College District, San Diego, California; **Vittoria G. Maghsoudi-Abbate**, Assistant Director, Mt. Diablo Adult Education, Mt. Diablo USD, Concord, California; **Irina Patten**, Lone Star College-Fairbanks Center, Houston, Texas; **Maria Soto Caratini**, Eastfield College DCCCD, Mesquite, Texas; **Claire Valier**, Palm Beach County, Florida; **Jacqueline S. Walpole**, Director, Adult Education, Prince George's Community College, Largo, Maryland.

Reviewers

Eleanor Brockman-Forfang, Instructor, Special Projects (ESL), Tarrant County College, South Campus, Fort Worth, TX; **Natalya Dollar**, ESL Program Resource Coordinator, North Orange County Community College District, Anaheim, CA; **Bette Empol**, ESL, ABE, GED Prep and Bridge Coordinator, Conejo Valley Adult School, Thousand Oaks, CA; **Mark Fisher**, Lone Star College-Fairbanks Center, Houston, TX; **Ann Fontanella**, ESL Instructor, City College of San Francisco, San Francisco, CA; **Ingrid Greenberg**, Associate Professor, ESL, and Past-President, Academic Senate, Continuing Education, San Diego Community College District, San Diego, CA; **Janet Harclerode**, Santa Monica College, Santa Monica, CA; **Laura Jensen**, ESL Instructor, North Seattle Community College, Seattle, WA; **Tommie Martinez**, Fresno Adult School, Fresno, CA; **Suzanne L. Monti**, ESOL Instructional Specialist, Community College of Baltimore County, Continuing Education, Baltimore, MD; **Kelly Nusz**, Carlos Rosario Charter School, Washington, D.C; **Irina Patten**, Lone Star College-Fairbanks Center, Houston, TX; **Ariel Peckokas**, Collier County Public Schools Adult Education, Naples, FL; **Sydney Rice**, Imperial Valley College, Imperial, CA; **Richard Salvador**, McKinley Community Schools of Arts, Honolulu, Hawaii; **Maria Soto Caratini**, Eastfield College DCCCD, Mesquite, TX; **Patty Swartzbaugh**, Nashville Adult Literacy Council, Nashville, TN; **Candace Thompson-Lynch**, ESL Instructor, School of Continuing Education, North Orange County Community College District, Anaheim, CA; **Esther M. Tillet**, Miami Dade College-Wolfson Campus, Miami, FL; **Adriana Treadway**, Assistant Director, Spring International Language Center, University of Arkansas, Fayetteville, AR; **Monica C. Vazquez**, ESOL Adjunct Instructor, Brookhaven College, DCCCD, Farmers Branch, TX.

AUTHOR / SERIES CONSULTANT

Sarah Lynn has over twenty-five years of teaching experience in ESOL. She has dedicated much of her teaching life to working with low-level learners with interrupted education. Currently she teaches at the Harvard Bridge Program, Harvard University. As a teacher trainer, Sarah has led professional development workshops throughout the United States on topics such as teaching in the multilevel classroom, learner persistence, twenty-first-century skills, self-directed learning, collaborative learning, and scaffolding learning for the literacy learner. As a consultant, she has written ESOL curricula for programs in civics, literacy, phonics, and English language arts. As a materials writer, she has contributed to numerous Pearson ELT publications, including *Business Across Cultures, Future, Future U.S. Citizens*, and *Project Success*. Sarah holds a master's degree in TESOL from Teacher's College, Columbia University.

SERIES CONSULTANT

Susan Gaer has worked as an ESL teacher since 1980 and currently teaches at the Santa Ana College School of Continuing Education. She is an avid user of technology and trains teachers online for TESOL and the Outreach Technical Assistance Center (OTAN). Susan is a frequent presenter at local, state, national, and international conferences on using the latest technology with adult learners from the literacy level through transition to college. She has co-authored books and teacher's manuals, served on the executive boards for CATESOL (California Teachers of English to Speakers of Other Languages) and TESOL, and contributed to standing committees for professional development and technology. Susan holds a master's degree in English with emphasis in TESOL from San Francisco State University and a master's degree in Educational Technology from Pepperdine University.

Scope and Sequence Intro

Unit	Listening/Speaking VIDEO	Grammar VIDEO	Practical Skills	Reading Skills
Welcome page 2	• Introduce yourself • Identify classroom objects and actions • Ask for repetition and clarification	NA	• Complete a classroom form	• Learn about the *Project Success* Student Book
1 **Marie's New Job** page 5	• Introduce yourself • Spell your name • present ID upon request • Talk about occupations	• Subject pronouns • *be*: present tense affirmative in full form, singular and plural	• Respond appropriately to common personal information questions • State country of origin • Complete a personal information form **Numeracy:** • State your phone number	• Employment kiosks **Reading strategy:** • Identify the topic
2 **Luka's Busy Schedule** page 19	• Discuss a basic work schedule • Discuss availability • Talk about the time of an event • Discuss a bus schedule **Pronunciation:** • Syllables: contracted forms of *be* • Number contrasts	• *be*: contractions • *be*: negative, singular and plural	• Numbers 10–100 • Read a work schedule • Talk about business hours **Numeracy:** • State and write digital clock times	• Study tips **Reading strategy:** • Retell the information
3 **Min's New Family Member** page 33	• Ask for someone on the phone • Talk about family • Describe feelings • Talk about age **Pronunciation:** • Rising intonation of *yes/no* questions	• Possessive adjectives • *be*: yes/no questions and short answers	• Identify immediate family members • Say and write months of the year • Write dates **Numeracy:** • Say and write ordinal numbers	• Asking the right questions (appropriateness of questions) **Reading strategy:** • Summarize with a graphic organizer
4 **Ana's Good Idea** page 47	• Talk about clothing • Ask about prices • Ask about locations at work • Identify basic problems with clothing **Pronunciation:** • Plural endings	• *How much* • Questions with *Where*	• Identify U.S. coins • Identify U.S. bills • Identify sizes and colors • Place an online order **Numeracy:** • item, color, size, quantity, price, total	• Dress codes **Reading strategy:** • Define key concepts
5 **Victor's Neighborhood Restaurant** page 61	• Identify and respond to questions about household problems • Talk about bills • Identify places in the neighborhood • Ask for and give directions	• The imperative • Prepositions of location	• Read and physically respond to safety signs • Address an envelope • Recognize post office items **Numeracy:** • Write a check	• Saving money at the supermarket **Reading strategy:** • Connect text to self

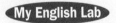

Vocabulary	Practical Skills	Writing	Unit Tests
Listening and Speaking	Grammar	Job-Seeking	Midterm Tests
Pronunciation	Reading		Final CASAS Test Prep

Writing Skills	Vocabulary ActiveTeach	Career Pathways	CASAS Highlights	Common Core College and Career Readiness
NA	• Classroom actions • Classroom objects			
• Describe yourself	• *First name, middle name, last name* • The alphabet • Countries • Forms of ID • Occupations • Titles	• Promote yourself in an interview • Develop interpersonal relationships • Manage others	0.1.1, 0.1.2, 0.1.4, 0.1.6, 0.1.7, 0.2.1, 0.2.2, 6.0.1, 6.0.2	R. 1, 2, 4, 7, 10 W. 2 SL. 1, 2, 3, 4, 6 L. 1, 2, 5 RF. 2, 4
• Write about your schedule	• Days of the week • Times of day • *Home, work, school* • Time • Events • *Early, on time, late*	• Deal with difficult situations • Negotiate • Mentor others • Demonstrate resilience • Communicate ideas clearly	0.1.1, 0.1.2, 0.1.3, 0.1.4, 0.1.6, 1.2.5, 2.2.4, 2.3.1, 2.3.2, 4.2.1, 4.4.1, 4.1.6, 4.4.3, 4.6.1, 4.8.6, 6.0.2, 6.6.6, 7.4.1	R. 5, 10 W. 2, 4 SL. 1, 2, 3, 4, 6 L. 1, 2, 5 RF. 2, 4
• Write about your family	• Family members • Feelings • Months • Ordinal numbers	• Manage your emotions • Develop interpersonal relationships • Communicate clearly • Exhibit patience	0.1.1, 0.1.2, 0.1.4, 0.1.8, 0.1.2, 0.1.4, 0.1.6, 0.2.1, 2.1.8, 2.3.2, 2.3.4, 6.0.1	R. 1, 2, 10 W. 2, 4 SL. 1, 2, 3, 4, 6 L. 1, 2, 5 RF. 2, 4
• Describe what you wear at work, home, school	• Clothing • U.S. coins • U.S. bills • Colors • Clothing sizes • Rooms at work • Problems with clothing • Dress codes	• Influence / persuade others • Sell an idea • Demonstrate resilience • Learn from mistakes	0.1.3, 0.1.4, 0.1.8, 1.1.6, 1.2.1, 1.2.2, 1.2.4, 1.2.5, 1.2.6, 1.2.7, 1.2.9, 1.3.1, 1.3.4, 4.6.1, 4.8.5, 6.1.1, 6.4.1, 6.5.1, 7.3.2	R. 1, 2, 4, 7, 10 W. 2, 4 SL. 1, 2, 3, 4, 6 L. 1, 2, 5 RF. 2, 4
• Write about your neighborhood	• Appliances • Safety signs • Business / household bills • Abbreviations in addresses • Places in the neighborhood • Post office items • Directions • Grocery store language	• Manage your emotions • Exhibit patience • Deal with difficult situations • Manage stress • Help others • Manage others	0.1.1, 0.1.2, 0.1.3, 0.1.4, 0.1.7, 0.1.8, 1.5.3, 1.7.3, 1.7.5, 2.2.1, 2.4.1, 2.4.4, 4.3.1, 4.5.1, 4.5.7, 4.6.1, 7.3.1	R. 1, 2, 10 W. 2, 4 SL. 1, 3, 4, 6 L. 1, 2, 5 RF. 2, 4

For complete correlations please visit www.pearsoneltusa.com/projectsuccess

Unit	Listening/Speaking VIDEO	Grammar VIDEO	Practical Skills	Reading Skills
6 **Marie's Customers** page 75	• Express likes and dislikes • Order food in a restaurant • Make and respond to a complaint • Request and make change	• simple present tense: *like, want, need, have*	• Identify foods • Identify containers • Read a menu • Talk about methods of payment	• Tipping **Reading strategy:** • Scanning
7 **Min Doesn't Feel Well** page 89	• Identify common ailments / Respond to a question about state of health • Identify medicines • Make an appointment • Call in sick **Pronunciation:** • Sentence rhythm	• Simple present tense: *yes/no* questions with *have* and *need* • Demonstratives	• Identify parts of the body • Read medicine labels • Respond physically to a doctor's commands • Read aisle numbers and locate items in a store	• A long and healthy life **Reading strategy:** • Skimming
8 **Ana's New Home** page 103	• Identify rooms in a home • Respond to simple questions about housing • Identify workplaces • Identify types of transportation **Pronunciation:** • Rising intonation on questions with *Is there* and *Are there*	• *There is/ There are* • *Is there / Are there* questions	• Describe your home • Identify furniture • Recognize bus signs • Recognize traffic signs	• A good neighborhood **Reading strategy:** • Listening for pauses in audio version of text (prosody)
9 **Luka Helps Out** page 117	• Apologize for being late • Offer to help • Simulate a 911 call and request appropriate assistance • Ask about people's activities	• Present Continuous • Present Continuous: *yes/no* questions	• Talk about the weather • Prepare for emergencies • Read signs related to health care • Leave a voicemail message • Read and understand a building directory	• Going to the emergency room **Reading strategy:** • Predicting
10 **Victor's Big Decisions** page 131	• Ask and answer questions about future employment goals • Talk about job skills • Talk about work experience • Congratulate someone **Pronunciation:** • *Can* and *Can't*	• *Can / can't* • *Can: yes/no* questions and short answers	• Find a job • Read an employment ad • Fill out a job application: personal information • Fill out a job application: employment history	• Volunteering **Reading strategy:** • Inferring

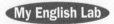

My English Lab

Vocabulary	Practical Skills	Writing	Unit Tests
Listening and Speaking	Grammar	Job-Seeking	Midterm Tests
Pronunciation	Reading		Final CASAS Test Prep

Writing Skills	Vocabulary ActiveTeach	Career Pathways	CASAS Highlights	Common Core College and Career Readiness
• Write about your favorite foods	• Food • Containers • Items on a menu • Meals • Methods of payment • More occupations • Fast foods	• Work as a team • Sell a product or idea • Influence / persuade others • Deal with difficult situations • Think on your feet	0.1.1, 0.1.2, 0.1.3, 0.1.4, 1.1.7, 1.2.5, 1.2.8, 1.3.1, 1.3.3, 2.6.4, 3.5.2, 4.8.3, 4.8.4, 4.8.6, 6.4.3, 6.5.1	R. 1, 2, 10 W. 2, 4 SL. 1, 3, 6 L. 1, 2, 5 RF. 2, 4
• Write about your remedies	• Parts of the body • The face • Ailments • Medicines • Medicine directions • Doctor's directions • Remedies • Items in a store	• Empathize / show concern • Ask for help • Communicate clearly • Manage others • Give advice	0.1.1, 0.1.2, 0.1.4, 0.1.7, 0.1.8, 0.2.1, 1.2.7, 2.1.8, 3.1.2, 3.1.3, 3.3.1, 3.5.9, 3.6.1, 3.6.3, 3.6.4	R. 2, 10 W. 2, 4 SL. 1, 2, 3, 4, 6 L. 1, 2, 5 RF. 2, 4
• Write about your home	• Buildings • Rooms in a home • Furniture • More occupations • Workplaces • Transportation • Traffic signs • *Quiet, loud*	• Demonstrate persistence and perseverance • Sell an idea • Influence / persuade others • Develop interpersonal relationships • Stress the positives in a situation	0.1.1, 0.1.2, 0.1.3, 0.1.4, 0.2.1, 1.4.1, 1.9.1, 2.2.2, 2.2.3, 4.1.6, 4.1.8	R. 1, 2, 3, 9, 10 W. 2, 4 SL. 1, 4, 6 L. 1, 2, 5 RF. 2, 4
• Write about your activities	• Weather • Chores • Emergencies • Places in a hospital • Activities	• Keep others informed • Manage others • Deal with difficult situations • Think and communicate on your feet • Function under pressure • Work as a team	0.1.1, 0.1.2, 0.1.4, 0.1.8, 2.1.2, 2.1.7, 2.1.8, 2.3.3, 2.5.1, 3.1.3, 3.1.4, 3.6.2, 4.8.1, 8.2.2, 8.2.3, 8.2.4, 8.2.6	R. 1, 2, 10 W. 2, 4 SL. 1, 2, 3, 4, 6 L. 1, 2, 5 RF. 2, 4
• Write about your goals for the future	• Ways to find out about jobs • More occupations • Abbreviations in employment ads • Job skills • Achievements	• Demonstrate leadership • Promote yourself • Mentor someone • Exhibit self-confidence • Promote yourself in an interview	0.1.1, 0.1.2, 0.1.4, 0.1.8, 0.2.1, 4.1.2, 4.1.3, 4.1.5, 4.1.6, 4.1.7, 4.1.8, 4.4.1, 4.4.2, 4.4.4, 4.4.7, 4.5.1, 7.5.1	R. 1, 2, 10 W. 2, 4 SL. 1, 2, 3, 4, 6 L. 1, 2, 4, 5 RF. 2, 4

To the Teacher

Project Success is a dynamic six-level, four-skills multimedia course for adults and young adults. It offers a comprehensive and integrated program for false-beginner to low-advanced learners, with a classroom and online curriculum correlated to national and state standards.

KEY FEATURES

In developing this course we focused on our students' future aspirations, and on their current realities. Through inspiring stories of adults working and mastering life's challenges, we illustrate the skills and competencies adult English language learners need to participate fully and progress in their roles at home, work, school, and in the community. To create versatile and dynamic learning tools, we integrate digital features such as video, audio, and an online curriculum into one unified and comprehensive course. The result is *Project Success*: the first blended digital course designed for adult-education English language learners.

MULTIMEDIA: INSIDE AND OUTSIDE THE CLASSROOM

All *Project Success* materials are technologically integrated for seamless independent and classroom learning. The user-friendly digital interface will appeal to students who are already technologically adept, while providing full support for students who have less computer experience.

In class, the teacher uses the **ActiveTeach** DVD-ROM to project the lessons on the board. Video, audio, flashcards, conversation frameworks, checklists, comprehension questions, and other learning material are all available at the click of a button. Students use their print **Student Book** as they participate in class activities, take notes, and interact in group work.

Outside of class, students access their Project Success **eText** to review the videos, audio, and eFlashcards from class. They use their **MyEnglishLab** access code to get further practice online with new listenings and readings, additional practice activities, and video-based exercises.

A VARIETY OF WORKFORCE AND LIFE SKILLS

Each level of *Project Success* presents a different cast of characters at a different workplace. In each book, students learn instrumental language, employment, and educational skills as they watch the characters interact with co-workers, customers, family, and friends. As students move through the series, level by level, they learn about six important sectors in today's economy: food service, hospitality, healthcare, higher education, business, and retail.

The language and skills involved in daily life range from following directions, to phone conversations, to helping customers, to asking permission to leave early. By representing a day in the life of a character, *Project Success* can introduce a diverse sampling of the content, language, and competencies involved in daily life and work. This approach allows students to learn diverse competencies and then practice them, in different settings and contexts, at different points in the curriculum.

VIDEO VIGNETTES

Each unit is organized around a series of short videos that follow one main character through his or her workday. In Listening and Speaking lessons, students watch the video together, see the character model a key competency in a realistic setting, and then practice the competency in pairs and groups. Discussion questions and group activities encourage students to identify and interpret the rich cultural content embedded in the video. The unit's grammar points are presented in the context of natural language in the video and then highlighted for more study and practice in a separate grammar lesson.

CRITICAL THINKING SKILLS

In the *What do you think?* activity at the end of nearly every lesson, students analyze, evaluate, infer, or relate content in the lesson to other contexts and situations.

A ROBUST ASSESSMENT STRAND

The series includes a rich assessment package that consists of unit review tests, midterms, and a CASAS-like final test. The tests assess students on CASAS objectives which are integrated into practical skills and listening strands.

The tests are available online or in a printable version on the ActiveTeach.

THE COMPONENTS:

ActiveTeach

This is a powerful digital platform for teachers. It blends a digital form of the Student Book with interactive whiteboard (IWB) software and printable support materials.

MyEnglishLab

This is a dynamic, easy-to-use online learning and assessment program that is integral to the *Project Success* curriculum. Original interactive activities extend student practice of vocabulary, listening, speaking, pronunciation, grammar, reading, writing, and practical skills from the classroom learning component.

eText

The eText is a digital version of the Student Book with all the audio and video integrated, and with a complete set of the pop-up eFlashcards.

WELCOME TO *PROJECT SUCCESS!*

Project Success is a six-level digital and print English program designed for you. It teaches English, employment, and learning skills for your success at work and school.

YOUR CLASSROOM LEARNING

Bring the Student Book to your classroom to learn new material and to practice with your classmates in groups. Every unit has:

- Four video-based lessons for your listening and speaking skills
- Four practical skills lessons
- Two grammar lessons
- One lesson for writing
- One lesson for reading
- One review page

YOUR ONLINE LEARNING

Your access code is on the front cover of your Student Book. Use the access code to go online. There you will find eText and MyEnglishLab.

Go to your eText to review what you learned in class. You can watch the videos again, listen to audio, and review the Vocabulary Flashcards.

Go to MyEnglishLab online to practice what you learned in class. MyEnglishLab has:

- Extra listening practice
- Extra reading practice
- Extra grammar practice
- Extra writing practice
- Extra practice of vocabulary skills
- Extra practice of life skills
- Additional video-based exercises
- "Record and compare," so you can record yourself and listen to your own pronunciation
- Instant feedback
- Job-seeking activities

Welcome Unit

A ◀)) **Listen. Listen and repeat.**

A: Hello. I'm Sue.

B: Hi. I'm Joe.

A: Nice to meet you.

B: Nice to meet you, too.

B **Walk around the room.**
Meet your classmates.

Hello. I'm _____.

Hi. I'm _____.

Nice to meet you.

Nice to meet you, too.

C ◀)) **Look at the form. Listen and point.**
Listen and repeat.

Name: *Pablo Diaz*

School: *Lakeview Community Adult School*

Teacher's name: *Sarah Lynn*

Class: *ESL 1A*   Room: *105*

D **Complete the form.**

Name: _____

School: _____

Teacher's name: _____

Class: _____ Room: _____

E **PAIRS** **Show your form to your partner.**

LEARN CLASSROOM LANGUAGE

A 🔊 **Listen and point. Listen and repeat.**

1. look

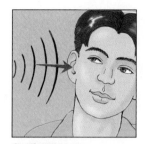

2. listen

3. point

4. repeat

5. read

6. write

7. open

8. close

B 🔊 **Listen and point. Listen and repeat.**

1. a chair

2. a table

3. a desk

4. a blackboard

5. a whiteboard

6. a book

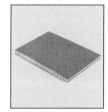

7. a notebook

8. a pen

9. a pencil

10. paper

C 🔊 **Listen and repeat.**

Please write your name.

Can you repeat that, please?

Turn to page 4.

What page?

Please turn on your computer.

I'm sorry. I don't understand.

LEARN ABOUT *PROJECT SUCCESS*

A **Learn about your book.**

1. Look at the cover of your book. What is the title of your book?

2. Look at the inside front cover. Point to the access code.

3. See page iii. How many units are in your book?

B **Meet the characters in your book. They work at Lakeside Café.**

I'm Victor Sánchez. I'm the owner and manager. Lakeside Café is my restaurant.

I'm Luka Petrov. I'm a dishwasher.

I'm Ana Sánchez. I'm the office assistant. I'm Victor's daughter.

I'm Marie Baptiste. I'm a new server.

I'm Min Lee. I'm a cook.

1 Marie's New Job

MY GOALS

Learn About:

- ☐ Introducing yourself
- ☐ Answering personal information questions
- ☐ Spelling your name
- ☐ Country of origin
- ☐ Showing an ID
- ☐ Phone numbers
- ☐ Occupations
- ☐ Personal information forms

Go to MyEnglishLab for more practice after each lesson.

Marie Baptiste
Marie   *Today*
I'm nervous. I have a job interview today.

Introduce yourself

GET READY TO WATCH

Marie is introducing herself.

What do you say to introduce yourself?

WATCH

 Watch the video. Match.

1. The restaurant is   **a.** Victor.

2. She is   **b.** Marie.

3. He is   **c.** Lakeside Café.

CONVERSATION

A 🔊)) **Listen and read. Listen and repeat.**

Victor: Hello. I'm Victor Sánchez.

Marie: Hi. I'm Marie Baptiste.

Victor: Nice to meet you.

Marie: Nice to meet you, too.

B **PAIRS** **Practice the conversation again. Use different ways to say _Hello_.**

A: _____. I'm _____.
       ★

B: _____. I'm _____.
       ★

A: Nice to meet you.

B: Nice to meet you, too.

ROLE PLAY

 GROUPS Watch the video again. Then introduce yourself to other classmates. Smile. Shake hands.

Hi. I'm _____.

Hello. I'm _____.

Nice to meet you.

Nice to meet you, too.

PRACTICAL SKILLS

Answer personal information questions

NAMES

A ◀)) **Listen and point. Listen and repeat.**

Victor _____ Manuel _____ Sánchez _____
first name   middle name   last name

B **Look at Exercise A. Answer the questions.**

1. What's his first name?   Victor _____

2. What's his middle name?   _____

3. What's his last name?   _____

C ◀)) **Listen and check your answers.**

D ◀)) **Listen and repeat.**

1. What's your first name?

2. What's your middle name?

3. What's your last name?

E **PAIRS** **Ask and answer the questions in Exercise D.**

F **Complete the form with your information.**

_____ _____ _____
first name   middle name   last name

WHAT ABOUT YOU?

A **Circle Yes or No for you.**

1. I have one first name.	Yes	No
2. I have two first names.	Yes	No
3. I have a middle name.	Yes	No
4. I have one last name.	Yes	No
5. I have two last names.	Yes	No

B **PAIRS** **Tell your partner about your names.**

I have two first names. My name is Mary Ann.

3 Spell your name

GET READY TO WATCH

Marie is at a job interview.

Guess. How does she feel?

WATCH

■◀ **Watch the video.**

Check [✓] the questions Victor asks.

☑ How do you spell your first name?

☐ What's your middle name?

☐ What's your last name?

☐ How do you spell your last name?

☐ Where are you from?

CONVERSATION

Ⓐ ◀))) **Listen and read. Listen and repeat.**

Victor: How do you spell your first name?

Marie: M-A-R-I-E.

Victor: How do you spell your last name?

Marie: B-A-P-T-I-S-T-E.

Victor: Thanks.

Ⓑ **PAIRS Practice the conversation again. Use your own names.**

A: How do you spell your first name?

B: _____.

A: How do you spell your last name?

B: _____.

A: Thanks.

WHAT ABOUT YOU?

GROUPS Ask and answer: How do you spell your first name?
How do you spell your last name?

How do you spell
your first name?

M-A-R-I-E.

Excuse me?

M-A-R-I-E.

Speaking Note

If you don't understand,
say: *Excuse me.*

PRACTICAL SKILLS

4

Talk about your country of origin

COUNTRIES

A **PAIRS** See the map on pages 162–163. **Point to your country. Say the name of your country.**

B ◄)) **Listen. Write the number of the conversation.**

_____ China	_____ the United States	_1_ Mexico
_____ Haiti	_____ Russia	_____ Brazil

C ◄)) **Listen and repeat.**

A: Where are you from?

B: I'm from Haiti.

A: Excuse me?

B: I'm from Haiti.

> **Language Note**
> Names of people and countries start with a capital letter.
> Marie   Haiti

D **PAIRS** **Practice conversation with your own country.**

A: Where are you from?

B: I'm from _____.

A: Excuse me?

B: I'm from _____.

WHAT ABOUT YOU?

GROUPS **Talk to 3 classmates. Complete the chart. Ask and answer:**

What's your name?
How do you spell it?
Where are you from?

Name	Country

What's your name?
Sarah.

Subject pronouns

 STUDY **Subject pronouns**

| I | you | he | she |

| we | they |

 PRACTICE

 **A** **Write.** (I   We)

1. ___I___ am from the U.S.   **2.** _____ are from the U.S.   **3.** _____ am from the U.S.

B ◀)) **Listen and check your answers.**

C **Write.** (He   She   They   He)

1. _____ is from New York.   **2.** _____ is from California.

3. _____ are from Florida.   **4.** _____ is from Texas.

D ◀)) **Listen and check your answers.**

PUT IT TOGETHER

PAIRS **Point to other classmates. Complete the sentence.**

_____ is from _____.   (She is from China.)   (He is from Brazil.)

LISTENING AND SPEAKING

Show an ID

 GET READY TO WATCH

Marie got the job! Now she is showing Victor an ID.

What kinds of ID do you have?

 WATCH

A ■◀ **Watch the video.**
Check [✓] the answers.

What forms of ID does Marie show Victor?

☐ a driver's license ☐ a Social Security card
☐ a passport ☐ a student ID

B ■◀ **Watch the video again. Circle the answer.**

What does Victor say before he leaves?

a. I'm going. **b.** I'll be right back.

 CONVERSATION

A ◀))) **Listen and read. Listen and repeat.**

Victor: May I see your ID?

Marie: Yes. Here's my driver's license.

Victor: Thanks. And do you have another ID?

Marie: Yes. Here's my Social Security card.

B PAIRS **Practice the conversation.**

C PAIRS **Practice the conversation again. Use different forms of ID.**

A: May I see your ID?

B: Yes. Here's my _____.
★

A: Thanks. And do you have another ID?

B: Yes. Here's my _____.
★

ROLE PLAY

■◀ PAIRS Watch the video again. Then act out the conversation.
Hand a "pretend" ID to your partner.

May I see your ID?

Yes. Here's my ____.

PRACTICAL SKILLS

Say your phone number

NUMBERS

◀))) **Listen and point. Listen and repeat.**

0   1   2   3   4   5   6   7   8   9

PHONE NUMBERS

Ⓐ ◀))) **Listen and point. Listen and repeat.**

1. a cell phone   **2. a home phone**

> **Speaking Note**
>
> For phone numbers:
> Say: *oh* or *zero* for 0.
> Say: the numbers in groups.
>
> ◀))) **Listen and repeat.**
> *(203) 555 - 1689*

(203) 555 - 1689

3. area   4. phone number
**   code**

Ⓑ ◀))) **Listen and write.**

1. cell phone __239__ - 555 - __6417__   home phone _____ - 555 - 1468

2. cell phone _____ - _____ - 4607   home phone _____ - 555 - _____

3. cell phone _____ - 555 - _____   home phone __X___

Ⓒ **Fill out the form. Then ask and answer.**

> Cell phone number: (_____) _____-_____
>
> Home phone number: (_____) _____-_____

> What's your cell
> phone number?

> What's your home
> phone number?

WHAT ABOUT YOU?

Ⓐ **Circle *Yes* or *No*.**

I have a cell phone.   Yes   No

I have a home phone.   Yes   No

Ⓑ **PAIRS Now tell a classmate.**   > I have a cell phone.

GET READY TO WATCH

Look at the picture. Guess.

Who is Marie talking to?

WATCH

A ■◀ **Watch the video. Was your guess correct?**

B ■◀ **Watch the video again. Circle the answer.**

Marie and Ana _____.

a. are friends

b. work at Lakeside Café

C ■◀ **Watch the video again. Check [✓] the jobs Marie and Ana talk about.**

☑ an office assistant

☐ a cook

☐ a sales assistant

☐ a manager

☐ a server

CONVERSATION

A ◀⟩⟩ **Listen and read. Listen and repeat.**

Marie: What do you do?

Ana: I am an office assistant.

B PAIRS **Practice the conversation.**

C PAIRS **Practice the conversation again. Use different occupations.**

Marie: What do you do?

Ana: I am a _____.
                              ★

WHAT ABOUT YOU?

GROUPS **Ask and answer:** What do you do?

What do you do?

I am a cook. And you?

I am a sales assistant.

Speaking Note

To continue the conversation, say: *And you?*

STUDY *Be*

I **am** a cook.	We **are** cooks.
You **are** a server.	You **are** servers.
He **is** a student.	They **are** students.
She **is** a student.	
Jen **is** a student.	

Grammar Note

a cook   cooks

 ## PRACTICE

A **Write.**

(am   is   are)

1. We ___*are*___ servers.

2. She _____ a cook.

3. You _____ students.

4. I _____ the manager.

5. He _____ a manager.

6. You _____ a teacher.

7. We _____ assistants.

8. They _____ cooks.

B **Write.**

(is   are)

1. Min ___*is*___ a cook.

2. Ana and Luka _____ students.

3. Victor _____ a manager.

4. Min and I _____ cooks.

5. Marie _____ a server.

6. Luka and I _____ dishwashers.

PUT IT TOGETHER

PAIRS Make sentences.

She	a teacher
I	a student
They	servers
Ana	an office assistant

She is a teacher.

PERSONAL INFORMATION

(A) **Look at the form. Whose information is on the form?**

Title: ☐ Mr.   ☐ Mrs.   ☑ Ms.   ☐ Miss

Marie   _Nicole_   _Baptiste_
First name   Middle name   Last name
Home phone: _(312) 555 -9807_ Cell phone: _(773) 555-4244_
Email address: _Marie07@kmail.com_
Occupation: _Server_   Employer: _Lakeside Café_
Signature: _Marie N. Baptiste_

(B) **Look at Exercise A. Match.**

1. What's Marie's occupation?   **a.** Marie07@kmail.com
2. What's Marie's cell phone number?   **b.** Server
3. What's Marie's email address?   **c.** (773) 555 - 4244
4. What's Marie's home phone number?   **d.** (312) 555 - 9807

(C) 🔊 **Listen and check your answers.**

(D) **Complete the form with your information.**

Title: ☐ Mr.   ☐ Mrs.   ☐ Ms.   ☐ Miss

First name   Middle name   Last name
Home phone: _____ Cell phone: _____
Email address: _____
Occupation: _____ Employer: _____
Signature: _____

WHAT ABOUT YOU?

GROUPS Ask 3 classmates: What's your email address?

> What's your email address?

Speaking Note

To say an email address:
@ = at   . = dot

🔊 **Listen and repeat.**
Marie07@kmail.com

GET READY

Where do you see employment kiosks?

READD

◀))) **Look at the title and picture. What is the reading about?**
Listen and read the article.

The Employment Kiosk

Many job applications are on employment kiosks. Employment kiosks are computers. How do you use an employment kiosk? Here are some tips.

1. At home, write down important information about your last job:
   - your job title (your occupation)
   - your employer (the name of the business)
   - your manager's name
   - your manager's phone number and email
2. Go to the business. Bring your information. Bring a friend to help with English.
3. Find the employment kiosk. Fill out the application. When you are done, you can leave. The employer will call you for a job interview.

CHECK YOUR UNDERSTANDING

Read again. Circle Yes or No.

1. A kiosk is a computer.	Yes	No
2. You can use a kiosk at home.	Yes	No
3. A friend can help you with the kiosk application.	Yes	No
4. Bring information about your last job to the kiosk.	Yes	No
5. Bring your manager to the kiosk.	Yes	No

WRITING

12 Describe yourself

STUDY THE MODEL

Read about Marie.

My name is Marie Baptiste.
I am from Haiti.
I am a server in a restaurant.
I work at Lakeside Café.

CHECK YOUR UNDERSTANDING

Write Marie's information.

Name: _Marie Baptiste_

Country: _____

Occupation: _____

Employer: _____

BEFORE YOU WRITE

A **Write your information.**

Name: _____

Country: _____

Occupation: _____

Employer: _____

B **Tell your partner about yourself.**

WRITE

**Complete the sentences about yourself. Use information from Exercise A.
Then copy the sentences on a separate piece of paper.**

My name is _____.

I am from _____.

I am a _____.

I work at _____.

I am a student at _____.

GRAMMAR

See page 145 for your Grammar Review.

VOCABULARY See page 155 for the Unit 1 Vocabulary.

Cross out the word that is different.

1. dishwasher	cook	server	~~teacher~~
2. he	they	ID	you
3. Brazil	English	Russia	China
4. passport	manager	driver's license	student ID
5. store	phone number	area code	cell phone
6. Mr.	Miss	Ms.	Mrs.

SPELLING See page 155 for the Unit 1 Vocabulary.

CLASS Choose 10 words for a spelling test.

LISTENING PLUS

 CLASS Watch each video.
Write the story of Marie's day on a separate piece of paper.

> _Marie has a job interview at the restaurant._

B PAIRS Choose one of these conversations.
Role play the conversation for the class.

Answer personal information questions. (See page 7.)

Talk about your country of origin. (See page 9.)

Talk about occupations. (See page 13.)

NOW I CAN

PAIRS See page 5 for the Unit 1 Goals. Check ☑ the things you can do.
Underline the things you want to study more. Tell your partner.

> I can _____. I need more practice with _____.

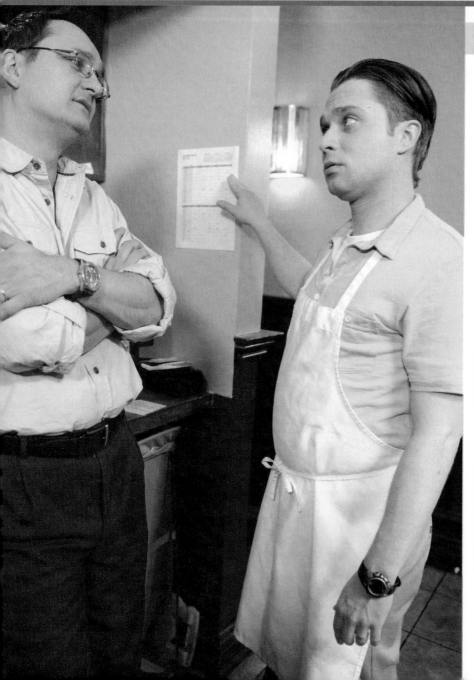

2 Luka's Busy Schedule

MY GOALS

Learn About:

☐ Work schedules

☐ Talking about availability

☐ Numbers 10–100

☐ Saying the time

☐ Giving the time of an event

☐ Business hours

☐ Bus schedules

Go to MyEnglishLab for more practice after each lesson.

Luka Petrov

Luka   *Today*

I am a father,
a student, and
a dishwasher.
I am busy!

Talk about work schedules

GET READY TO WATCH

Luka is reading his schedule. He is not happy.
Are you happy with your work schedule?

WATCH

A ◼◀ **PAIRS** **Watch the video.**
What is Luka's problem?

B ◼◀ **Watch the video again. Read the question. Circle the days.**

1. When is Min at work next week?

   Sunday   Monday   Tuesday   Wednesday   Thursday   Friday   Saturday

2. When is Luka at work next week?

   Sunday   Monday   Tuesday   Wednesday   Thursday   Friday   Saturday

3. When is Luka at school?

   Sunday   Monday   Tuesday   Wednesday   Thursday   Friday   Saturday

CONVERSATION

A ◀))) **Listen and read. Listen and repeat.**

Luka: What's your schedule?

Min: I work on Sunday, Monday, Tuesday, Thursday, and Saturday.
I'm off on Wednesday and Friday.

B **PAIRS** **Practice the conversation.**

C **PAIRS** **Practice the conversation again. Talk about different days.**

A: What's your schedule?

B: I work on _____.
★

I'm off on _____.
★

ROLE PLAY

PAIRS **Ask and answer:** What's your class schedule?
Then ask and answer with another partner.

What's your class
schedule?

I'm in class on _____.
I'm off on _____.

GRAMMAR

2 *Be:* Contractions

STUDY *Be:* Contractions

Full Form	Contraction	
I am →	**I'm**	**I'm** off on Tuesday.
you are →	**you're**	**You're** off on Tuesday.
she is →	**she's**	**She's** off on Tuesday.
he is →	**he's**	**He's** off on Tuesday.
we are →	**we're**	**We're** off on Tuesday.
they are →	**they're**	**They're** off on Tuesday.

Pronunciation Note

The contractions of *be* are one syllable.

◀)) **Listen and repeat.**

I am	I'm
You are	You're
She is	She's
He is	He's
We are	We're
They are	They're

PRACTICE

A **Write the contraction.**

1. I am _I'm_

2. she is _____

3. you are _____

4. they are _____

5. he is _____

6. we are _____

B **Circle the word. Write the word.**

1. My name is Victor. ___*I'm*___ at the restaurant six days a week.
(I'm)/ I

2. Ana and I are off two days a week. _____ off on Monday and Tuesday.
We're / We

3. Ana is here five days a week. She _____ off two days a week.
is / She's

4. Luka is at the restaurant five days a week. He _____ here Monday to Friday.
He's / is

5. Marie and Luka are off on Sunday. _____ here on Monday.
They / They're

C ◀)) **Listen and check your answers. Listen again and repeat.**

PUT IT TOGETHER

PAIRS Make sentences. Use contractions.

I	here on Monday
She	off on weekends
We	here from Tuesday to Saturday
He	off on Friday
They	at the restaurant on Thursday

I'm here on Monday.

LESSON 3 LISTENING AND SPEAKING

Talk about availability

GET READY TO WATCH

Victor and Luka are talking.
Guess. What are they talking about?

WATCH

A ◼◀ Watch the video. Was your guess correct?

B ◼◀ Watch the video again. Circle the answer.

1. There's a problem with _____.
   a. the schedule   **b.** Victor

2. Victor will _____.
   a. work on weekends   **b.** fix the schedule

C ◼◀ Watch the video again. Circle *Yes* or *No*.

1. Is Luka available on Mondays?   Yes   No

2. Is Luka available on Saturdays?   Yes   No

3. Is Luka available on Sundays?   Yes   No

CONVERSATION

A ◀)) Listen and read. Listen and repeat.

Luka: I'm not available on weekends.

Victor: You're not? When are you available?

Luka: I'm available on weekdays.

B PAIRS Practice the conversation.

C PAIRS Practice the conversation again. Talk about different days.

A: I'm not available on _____.
   ★

B: You're not? When are you available?

A: I'm available on _____.
   ★

WHAT DO YOU THINK?

◼◀ PAIRS Watch the video again. Luka says, "I'm not available."
Is that a good idea?

I think . . .

Be: Negative

 STUDY *Be:* Negative

Full Form		Contraction	
I **am not**	→	I**'m not**	I**'m not** at work.
you **are not**	→	you**'re not**	You**'re not** at work.
she **is not**	→	she**'s not**	She**'s not** at work.
he **is not**	→	he**'s not**	He**'s not** at work.
we **are not**	→	we**'re not**	We**'re not** at work.
they **are not**	→	they**'re not**	They**'re not** at work.

PRACTICE

A **Complete the sentences with *be* + *not*.**

1. I ___am not___ available at night.

2. You _____ here on Sundays.

3. He _____ off on weekends.

4. We _____ here on Fridays.

5. They _____ off on Mondays.

B **Copy the sentences on a separate piece of paper. Use contractions.**

C **Look at the availability chart. Circle the word. Write the word.**

	Sunday	Monday	Tuesday	Wednesday	Thursday	Friday	Saturday
Luka	✗	✓	✓	✓	✓	✓	✗
Marie	✗	✓	✓	✓	✗	✓	✓

1. Luka ___is not___ available on Saturdays.
　　　　is /(is not)

2. Luka and Marie ___are___ available on Mondays.
　　　　　　　　　is /(are)

3. Marie _____ available on Saturdays.
　　　　is / is not

4. Luka and Marie _____ available on Sundays.
　　　　　　　　　are / are not

5. Marie _____ available on Thursdays.
　　　　is not / are not

PUT IT TOGETHER

PAIRS Make sentences in the negative.

She	available on weekends
I	here on Mondays
They	at the restaurant on Tuesdays

> She's not available on weekends.

PRACTICAL SKILLS

5

Numbers 10–100

NUMBERS

A ◀))) **Listen and point. Listen and repeat.**

10	11	12	13	14	15	16	17	18	19

B ◀))) **Listen and point. Listen and repeat.**

20	21	22	23	24	25	26	27	28	29
30	31	32	33	34	35	36	37	38	39

C ◀))) **Listen and point. Listen and repeat.**

10	20	30	40	50	60	70	80	90	100

D **PAIRS** **Student A:** Say a number. **Student B:** Point to the number.

E ◀))) **Listen and circle.**

a. 13   (30)   e. 17   70

b. 14   40   f. 18   80

c. 15   50   g. 19   90

d. 16   60

> **Pronunciation Note**
>
> These numbers have different endings.
>
> ◀))) **Listen and repeat.**
>
> | 13 thirteen | 30 thirty |
> |-------------|-----------|
> | 14 fourteen | 40 forty |
> | 15 fifteen | 50 fifty |
> | 16 sixteen | 60 sixty |

F ◀))) **Listen and write.**

a. _42_   e. ___   i. ___

b. ___   f. ___   j. ___

c. ___   g. ___   k. ___

d. ___   h. ___   l. ___

G **Write the answers.**

1. Number of days in a week: ___
2. Number of days in a year: ___
3. Number of hours in a day: ___
4. Number of weeks in a year: ___
5. Number of hours in a week: ___
6. Number of weekdays in a week: ___

WHAT ABOUT YOU?

GROUPS **Ask 3 classmates:** What's your lucky number?

What's your lucky number?

My lucky number is eight.

6

Say the time

TIME

A ◀)) **Listen and point. Listen and repeat.**

1. `10:00`   2. `10:05`   3. `10:10`   4. `10:15`

5. `10:20`   6. `10:25`   7. `10:30`   8. `10:35`

9. `10:40`   10. `10:45`   11. `10:50`   12. `10:55`

B **PAIRS** **Student A:** Say a time.
Student B: Point to the clock.

C ◀)) **Listen and write the times.**

1. ___4:30___   3. _____   5. _____

2. _____   4. _____   6. _____

D ◀)) **PAIRS** **Listen and repeat.**

A: Excuse me. What time is it?

B: It's 12:30.

A: 12:30?

B: Yes.

A: Thank you.

E **PAIRS** **Practice the conversation.**

A: Excuse me. What time is it?

B: It's ___.

A: Thank you.

> **Speaking Note**
>
> To check that you understand, repeat the other person's words as a question.
>
> ◀)) **Listen and repeat.**
>
> **A:** It's 12:30.
>
> **B:** 12:30?

WHAT ABOUT YOU?

GROUPS **Ask and answer:** How do you keep time?

with a watch

with a cell phone

with a clock

How do you keep time?

With a cell phone.

LISTENING AND SPEAKING

Give the time of an event

GET READY TO WATCH

Luka is on his break.
What is he doing?

WATCH

A ■◄ **Watch the video.**
Circle Yes or No.

1. Luka's break is at 2:45.   Yes   No
2. Luka is sleeping on his break.   Yes   No
3. Luka is tired.   Yes   No

B ■◄ **Watch the video again. Circle the answer.**

1. Ana says, "Your break is over." What does she mean?

   a. It's time for your break.   **b.** It's time to work.

2. What time does Luka wake up?

   a. 2:50.   **b.** 2:45.

CONVERSATION

A ◄))) **Listen and read. Listen and repeat.**

Ana: When is your break?

Luka: At 2:15.

B **PAIRS** **Practice the conversation.**

C **PAIRS** **Practice the conversation again.**
Talk about different events and times.

A: When is your _____?
                        ★

B: At _____.
        ★ ★

WHAT DO YOU THINK?

■◄ **PAIRS** Watch the video again. Luka falls asleep at work. Is that OK?

I think . . .

WORK SCHEDULES

A **Read the work schedule.**
Whose schedule is it?

Name: Luka Romanov
Week from: 12/3/16 to: 12/9/16

	Sun.	Mon.	Tues.	Wed.	Thur.	Fri.	Sat.	
In		5:00 P.M.	2:30 P.M.	2:30 P.M.	2:30 P.M.	2:30 P.M.		
Out		10:00 P.M.	10:30 P.M.	10:30 P.M.	10:30 P.M.	10:30 P.M.		
Total		5.0	8.0	8.0	8.0	8.0		37.0

B **Look at Exercise A. Circle Yes or No.**

1. Luka works 8 hours on Wednesdays.   Yes   No

2. Luka works from 2:30 to 10:30 on Thursdays.   Yes   No

3. Luka works a total of 34 hours every week.   Yes   No

C **Read. Complete Ana's work schedule.**

I work on Sundays from 10:00 A.M. to 4:00 P.M.

I work on Wednesdays and Thursdays from 10:30 A.M. to 6:30 P.M.

I work on Fridays and Saturdays from 12:00 P.M. to 8:00 P.M.

Name: Ana Sánchez
Week from: 12/3/16 to: 12/9/16

	Sun.	Mon.	Tues.	Wed.	Thur.	Fri.	Sat.	
In	10:00 A.M.							
Out								
Total								

WHAT ABOUT YOU?

GROUPS **Ask and answer:** What's your favorite time of day?

morning	evening
afternoon	night

What's your favorite
time of day?

My favorite time of
day is morning.

Talk about business hours

BUSINESS HOURS

A) Read the hours. Circle *Yes* or *No*.

1.

Store Hours				
Mon.	9:00 A.M.	to	8:00 P.M.	
Tues.	9:00 A.M.	to	8:00 P.M.	
Wed.	9:00 A.M.	to	8:00 P.M.	
Thur.	9:00 A.M.	to	8:00 P.M.	
Fri.	9:00 A.M.	to	8:00 P.M.	
Sat.	9:00 A.M.	to	8:00 P.M.	
Sun.	Closed	to	Closed	

1. The store is open on weekdays.
   Yes   No

2. It is open at 9:00 on Thursday morning.
   Yes   No

3. It is open at 7:00 on Friday evening.
   Yes   No

4. The store is closed on Saturday.
   Yes   No

2.

Restaurant Hours
Monday: Closed
Tuesday–Saturday 11:00 A.M.–10:00 P.M.
Sunday 10:00 A.M.–4:00 P.M.

1. The restaurant is open on Monday.
   Yes   No

2. It is closed on Sunday night.
   Yes   No

3. It is open on Wednesday afternoon.
   Yes   No

4. It is closed on Tuesday morning at 9:00.
   Yes   No

B) ◄)) Listen and complete the hours.

1. Monday _9:00 A.M._ – _5:00 P.M._

2. Tuesday _____ – _____

3. Wednesday _____ – _____

4. Thursday _____ – _____

5. Friday _____ – _____

6. Saturday _____ – _____

7. Sunday _____

WHAT ABOUT YOU?

GROUPS **Ask and answer:** How do you find out business hours?

I call.

I read the sign.

I look online.

How do you find out
business hours?

I look online.

LISTENING AND SPEAKING

Talk about a bus schedule

 GET READY TO WATCH

Luka is in a hurry.

Guess. Where is he going?

 WATCH

A 🎥 **Watch the video.**
Was your guess correct?

B 🎥 **Watch the video again.**
Circle the answer.

1. It's ____.	**a.** morning	**b.** evening
2. The bus is at ____.	**a.** 10:45	**b.** 11:10
3. The next bus is at ____.	**a.** 12:00	**b.** 11:15

C 🎥 **Watch the video again. Circle _Yes_ or _No_.**

1. Luka is late for the first bus.	Yes	No
2. Luka is early for the next bus.	Yes	No

 CONVERSATION

A 🔊 **Listen and read. Listen and repeat.**

Luka: I have to catch my bus. What time is it?

Victor: It's 10:45.

Luka: Oh, no. I'm late.

B **PAIRS Practice the conversation.**

C **PAIRS Practice the conversation again. Use different times.**

A: I have to catch my bus. What time is it?

B: It's _____.
　　　　　　★

A: _____.
　　★★

▶ ROLE PLAY

PAIRS Practice the conversation again. Talk about a class.

I have to go to class. What time is it?

It's 9:00.

Oh, good. I'm on time.

When do you study?

 READ

◄))) **Listen and read the study tips. Who is writing the tips?**

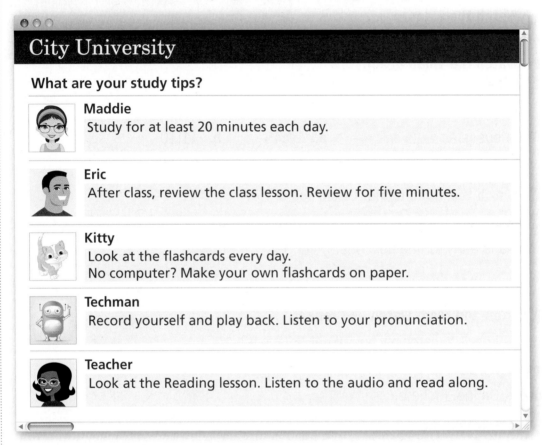

City University

What are your study tips?

Maddie
Study for at least 20 minutes each day.

Eric
After class, review the class lesson. Review for five minutes.

Kitty
Look at the flashcards every day.
No computer? Make your own flashcards on paper.

Techman
Record yourself and play back. Listen to your pronunciation.

Teacher
Look at the Reading lesson. Listen to the audio and read along.

 CHECK YOUR UNDERSTANDING

Read again. Write.   (Look   Listen   Review   Record   Study)

1. _____ yourself. Then listen to your pronunciation.

2. _____ at the flashcards every day.

3. _____ the lesson after class.

4. _____ to the audio as you read.

5. _____ 20 minutes every day.

Write about your schedule

 STUDY THE MODEL

Read the email message.

 Luka Petrov
to Peter Banks

Hi, Peter,

How are you? I'm fine, but I'm very busy. I study at home on weekdays from 8:00 to
12:00. I'm at work on Mondays from 5:00 to 10:00, and on Tuesdays, Wednesdays,
Thursdays, and Fridays from 2:30 to 10:30. I'm at school on Saturdays and Sundays.

Best,

Luka

 CHECK YOUR UNDERSTANDING

Read again. Complete the schedule. Use *at work*, *at home*, and *at school*.

Sunday	Monday	Tuesday	Wednesday	Thursday	Friday	Saturday
		2:30–10:30 at work				

 BEFORE YOU WRITE

Complete your schedule.

Sunday	Monday	Tuesday	Wednesday	Thursday	Friday	Saturday

 WRITE

Complete the sentences. Use your schedule.
Then copy the sentences on a separate piece of paper.

I'm at school on _____ from _____ to _____.

I'm at work on _____ from _____ to _____.

I'm at home on _____ from _____ to _____.

GRAMMAR

See page 146 for your Grammar Review.

VOCABULARY See page 155 for the Unit 2 Vocabulary.

Write words for each group. Tell a classmate your words.

Weekends	Weekdays	Times of day	Places to be
Saturday	Monday	morning	school

SPELLING See page 155 for the Unit 2 Vocabulary.

CLASS Choose 10 words for a spelling test.

LISTENING PLUS

Ⓐ CLASS Watch each video.
Write the story of Luka's day on a separate piece of paper.

Luka has a busy schedule.

Ⓑ PAIRS Choose one of these conversations.
Role play the conversation for the class.

Talk about work schedules. (See page 20.)

Say the time. (See page 25.)

Talk about a bus schedule. (See page 29.)

NOW I CAN

PAIRS See page 19 for the Unit 2 Goals. Check ☑ the things you can do.
Underline the things you want to study more. Tell your partner.

I can _____. I need more practice with _____.

3 Min's New Family Member

MY GOALS

Learn About:

- ☐ Asking for someone on the phone
- ☐ Family members
- ☐ Feelings
- ☐ Months of the year
- ☐ Saying dates
- ☐ Writing dates
- ☐ Talking about age

Go to MyEnglishLab for more practice after each lesson.

Min Lee

Min *Today*
I'm so happy. There's a new baby in our family!

LISTENING AND SPEAKING

1 Ask for someone on the phone

GET READY TO WATCH

Marie is answering the phone.
How do you answer the phone?
What do you say?

WATCH

A ■◄ **Watch the video.**
Circle the answer.

What is Min waiting for?

a. Her daughter.   **b.** A phone call.

B ■◄ **Watch the video again. Write.**

(Min   Tom Lee   Marie)

1. The call is for _____Min_____.

2. _____ calls the restaurant.

3. _____ answers the phone.

4. _____ is worried about her daughter.

CONVERSATION

A ◄))) **Listen and read. Listen and repeat.**

Marie: Lakeside Café. This is Marie.

Tom: Hello. This is Tom Lee. May I speak to Min?

Marie: Yes. One minute, please.

B **PAIRS** **Practice the conversation with your names.**

A: Lakeside Café. This is _____.

B: Hello. This is _____. May I speak to _____?

A: Yes. One minute, please.

WHAT DO YOU THINK?

■◄ **PAIRS** Watch the video again. Guess. What does Tom tell Min?

(I think . . .)

PRACTICAL SKILLS

Family members

FAMILY MEMBERS

A 🔊 **Listen and point. Listen and repeat.**

1. grandparents
2. grandfather   3. grandmother
4. parents
5. mother   6. father
7. children
8. son   9. daughter

10. wife   11. husband

12. brother   13. sister

14. grandson   15. granddaughter

B **Write.**

(grandson   mother   parents   ~~sister~~   son)

1. I have a _____*sister*_____. She's a sales assistant.
2. I have two children: a daughter and a _____.
3. My _____ are in Los Angeles.
4. My parents work at a restaurant. My _____ is a cook, and my father is a server.
5. My daughter has a son. He is my only _____.

C 🔊 **Listen and check your answers. Listen again and repeat.**

WHAT ABOUT YOU?

PAIRS Tell your partner about your family.

(I have a brother and a sister.)

LISTENING AND SPEAKING

Talk about family

GET READY TO WATCH

Min is very happy.
Guess. Why is she happy?

WATCH

A ■◄ **Watch the video.**
Was your guess correct?

B ■◄ **Watch the video again. Circle *Yes* or *No*.**

1. Min has a baby boy.   Yes   No

2. Min is a grandmother.   Yes   No

3. Min has two grandchildren.   Yes   No

C ■◄ **Watch the video again. Circle the answer.**

What do people say when someone has a baby?

a. Congratulations.   **b.** You're welcome.

CONVERSATION

A ◄))) **Listen and read. Listen and repeat.**

Marie: Who's that?

Min: That's my granddaughter.

B **PAIRS** **Practice the conversation.**

C **PAIRS** **Show your partner photos of your family.**

Student A: Point to a photo. Ask the question.

Student B: Answer the question.

A: Who's that?

B: That's my _____.

WHAT ABOUT YOU?

PAIRS Say more about your family members.

Who's that?

That's my sister. She's a cook. She's in Brazil.

Possessive adjectives

STUDY Possessive adjectives

I	→	my	**My** name is Min.
you	→	**your**	**Your** name is Marie.
he	→	**his**	**His** name is Sam.
she	→	**her**	**Her** name is Lisa.
we	→	**our**	**Our** last name is Park.
they	→	**their**	**Their** last name is Cueva.

PRACTICE

A **Write. Use words from the box.**   Her   His   ~~my~~   Our   Their

This is my family.

Sonine Baptiste   Yanick Baptiste   Joey Baptiste   Joseph Baptiste

1. This is ____my____ family.
2. That's my brother. He is a student. _____ name is Joey.
3. That's my sister. She is a teacher. _____ name is Yanick.
4. They are my parents. _____ names are Sonine and Joseph.
5. We all have the same last name. _____ last name is Baptiste.

B **Circle the word. Write the word.**

1. I have six brothers. ____My____ family is big.
2. He has a little sister. _____ little sister is a baby.
3. They have two girls. _____ daughters are students.
4. She is a restaurant owner. _____ restaurant is in Miami.
5. We have five grandchildren. _____ grandchildren live in Texas.

WHAT ABOUT YOU?

PAIRS Show your partner photos of your family.
Look at your partner's photos. Ask and answer the questions.

Who's that?

That's my son.

What's his name?

His name is John.

5

Describe feelings

GET READY TO WATCH

Min is talking to her daughter, Jenny.

Guess. Min is ____.

a. tired   **b.** worried   **c.** sad

WATCH

A   ◼◀ **Watch the video.**
Check [✓] the people Min asks about.

☐ her daughter   ☐ her granddaughter
☐ her son   ☐ her grandson

B   ◼◀ **Watch the video again. Circle the answer.**

How does Jenny answer her cell phone?

a. Hello?   **b.** Hello. This is Jenny.

CONVERSATION

A   ◀)) **Listen and read. Listen and repeat.**

Min: Are you OK?

Jenny: Yes. I'm fine.

Speaking Note

Use rising intonation for
yes/no questions.

◀)) **Listen and repeat.**

Are you ͟OK?

B   **PAIRS** **Practice the conversation.**

C   **PAIRS** **Imagine you are talking to a close friend. Practice the conversation 2 more times. First, answer yes. Then, answer *no*.**

A: Are you OK?

B: Yes. I'm _____.
⭐

A: Are you OK?

B: No. I'm _____.
⭐⭐

ROLE PLAY

GROUPS Practice the conversation with more classmates.
Say *And you?* to continue the conversation.

> Are you OK?
>> Yes. I'm fine. And you?
> I'm OK.

GRAMMAR

6

Be: Yes/no questions

STUDY *Be: Yes/no questions*

Questions	Answers	
Are you tired?	Yes, **I am**.	No, **I'm not**.
Is she tired?	Yes, **she is**.	No, **she's not**.
Is he tired?	Yes, **he is**.	No, **he's not**.
Is Kate tired?	Yes, **she is**.	No, **she's not**.
Are you tired?	Yes, **we are**.	No, **we're not**.
Are they tired?	Yes, **they are**.	No, **they're not**.

PRACTICE

A **Match.**

1. Is Min at the hospital?   **a.** Yes, they are.

2. Is Sam hungry?   **b.** No, I'm not.

3. Are Min and Jenny happy?   **c.** Yes, he is.

4. Are you OK?   **d.** No, she's not.

B **Write.**

1. **A:** _____Are_____ you worried?

   B: No, _____I'm_____ not.

2. **A:** Is she happy?

   B: Yes, _____ _____.

3. **A:** _____ they tired?

   B: Yes, they are.

4. **A:** Is he here?

   B: No, _____ not.

5. **A:** Are you OK?

   B: Yes, I _____.

6. **A:** _____ they sad?

   B: No, they're not.

7. **A:** _____ she OK?

   B: No, she's not.

8. **A:** Is he tired?

   B: Yes, _____ _____.

C 🔊 **Listen and check your answers.**
   Then practice the conversations with a partner.

PUT IT TOGETHER

PAIRS Look at the pictures on the screen. Ask and answer questions about the people.

Is she happy?

Yes, she is.

Is he tired?

No, he's not.

PRACTICAL SKILLS

Months of the year

MONTHS

A ◀))) **Listen and point. Listen and repeat.**

January	February	March	April
	1 2 3	1 2 3 4 5 6 7	1 2 3 4 5 6 7	1 2 3 4
4 5 6 7 8 9 10	8 9 10 11 12 13 14	8 9 10 11 12 13 14	5 6 7 8 9 10 11
11 12 13 14 15 16 17	15 16 17 18 19 20 21	15 16 17 18 19 20 21	12 13 14 15 16 17 18
18 19 20 21 22 23 24	22 23 24 25 26 27 28	22 23 24 25 26 27 28	19 20 21 22 23 24 25
25 26 27 28 29 30 31		29 30 31	26 27 28 29 30

May	June	July	August
	1 2	1 2 3 4 5 6	1 2 3 4	1
3 4 5 6 7 8 9	7 8 9 10 11 12 13	5 6 7 8 9 10 11	2 3 4 5 6 7 8
10 11 12 13 14 15 16	14 15 16 17 18 19 20	12 13 14 15 16 17 18	9 10 11 12 13 14 15
17 18 19 20 21 22 23	21 22 23 24 25 26 27	19 20 21 22 23 24 25	16 17 18 19 20 21 22
24 25 26 27 28 29 30	28 29 30	26 27 28 29 30 31	23 24 25 26 27 28 29
31			30 31

September	October	November	December
	1 2 3 4 5	1 2 3	1 2 3 4 5 6 7	1 2 3 4 5
6 7 8 9 10 11 12	4 5 6 7 8 9 10	8 9 10 11 12 13 14	6 7 8 9 10 11 12
13 14 15 16 17 18 19	11 12 13 14 15 16 17	15 16 17 18 19 20 21	13 14 15 16 17 18 19
20 21 22 23 24 25 26	18 19 20 21 22 23 24	22 23 24 25 26 27 28	20 21 22 23 24 25 26
27 28 29 30	25 26 27 28 29 30 31	29 30	27 28 29 30 31

B **PAIRS** **Student A:** Say a month. **Student B:** Point to the month.

C ◀))) **Listen and circle.**

1. (January)   February

2. April   August

3. March   May

4. November   December

5. June   July

6. September   October

D ◀))) **Listen and write.**

1. _February_

2. _____

3. _____

4. _____

5. _____

6. _____

WHAT ABOUT YOU?

GROUPS **Ask 3 classmates:** What's your favorite month?

What's your favorite month?

My favorite month is . . .

PRACTICAL SKILLS

Talk about today's date

A ◀))) ORDINAL NUMBERS

Listen and point. Listen and repeat.

1st first	11th eleventh	21st twenty-first	40th fortieth
2nd second	12th twelfth	22nd twenty-second	50th fiftieth
3rd third	13th thirteenth	23rd twenty-third	60th sixtieth
4th fourth	14th fourteenth	24th twenty-fourth	70th seventieth
5th fifth	15th fifteenth	25th twenty-fifth	80th eightieth
6th sixth	16th sixteenth	26th twenty-sixth	90th ninetieth
7th seventh	17th seventeenth	27th twenty-seventh	100th one hundredth
8th eighth	18th eighteenth	28th twenty-eighth	
9th ninth	19th nineteenth	29th twenty-ninth	
10th tenth	20th twentieth	30th thirtieth	

B **PAIRS** **Student A:** Say an ordinal number. **Student B:** Point to the number.

C ◀))) **Listen and circle.**

1. (January 2nd) January 22nd
2. September 5th September 15th
3. August 13th August 30th
4. July 1st July 21st
5. March 4th March 14th
6. April 16th April 26th

D ◀))) **Listen and repeat.**

A: What's today's date?

B: It's October 23rd.

A: Could you repeat that, please?

B: It's October 23rd.

> **Speaking Note**
>
> To ask someone to repeat, you can say: *Could you repeat that, please?*

ROLE PLAY

PAIRS Practice the conversation. First use today's date. Then use other dates.

A: What's today's date?

B: It's _____.

A: Could you repeat that, please?

B: It's _____.

PRACTICAL SKILLS

9 Write dates

DATES

A Number the months 1–12.

_1_ – January	_2_ – February	_3_ – March	____ – April
____ – May	____ – June	____ – July	____ – August
____ – September	____ – October	____ – November	____ – December

B Match.

month / day / year

1. April 12, 2017   6/3/19
2. June 3, 2019   12/31/81
3. August 23, 2004   4/12/17
4. December 31, 1981   8/23/04

C Write.

month / day / year

1. July 4, 2016   _7_ / _4_ / _16_
2. May 5, 1965   ____ / ____ / _____
3. October 21, 1999   ____ / ____ / _____
4. November 30, 2019   ____ / ____ / _____
5. September 12, 2014   ____ / ____ / _____

Speaking Note

Write **March 1**. Say *March first*.
Write **March 2**. Say *March second*.
Write **March 3**. Say *March third*.

D Read the form. Then complete the form with your information.

Name: _James_ _Cross_   Date of birth: _11/23/94_
     first   last

Name: _____   Date of birth: _____
    first   last

WHAT DO YOU THINK?

PAIRS Is your date of birth personal information?

I think . . .

LISTENING AND SPEAKING

Talk about age

GET READY TO WATCH

Min is putting candles on a birthday cake.

Do you have birthday cake on your birthday?

WATCH

A   ◼◀ **Watch the video. Circle *Yes* or *No*.**

1. The birthday cake is for a customer.   Yes   No

2. Tomorrow is Luka's birthday.   Yes   No

3. Luka has a grandson.   Yes   No

B   ◼◀ **Watch the video again. Circle the answer.**

1. Why does Luka say, "Congratulations" to Min?

   a. It's her birthday.   **b.** She has a new grandson.

2. Today is a customer's birthday. What do the restaurant employees do?

   a. They say, "Congratulations!"   **b.** They sing "Happy Birthday."

CONVERSATION

A   ◀)) **Listen and read. Listen and repeat.**

Min: How old is your daughter?

Luka: She's four years old.

B   **PAIRS** **Practice the conversation.**

C   **PAIRS** **Practice the conversation again. Talk about your family.**

A: How old is your _____?
            ★

B: _____ _____ years old.
    ★★

WHAT ABOUT YOU?

GROUPS **Ask 3 classmates:** When is your birthday?

When is your birthday?

    It's April 14th.

Asking the right questions

GET READY

In your country, is it OK to ask your classmates these questions?

1. How old are you?   OK   Not OK

2. When is your birthday?   OK   Not OK

3. What's your date of birth? OK   Not OK

READP

◀)) **Listen and read the article. Circle all the questions.**

Living in the U.S.: Asking the Right Questions

Is it OK to ask, "How old are you?"
Sometimes it's OK. Sometimes it's not OK.
✓ It's OK to ask children.
✓ It's OK to ask close friends.
✗ It's not OK to ask adults you are not close to.
✗ It's not OK to ask in a job interview.

Is it OK to ask, "When is your birthday?"
✓ Yes. Birthdays are important in the United States. People
   want to say "Happy Birthday" to you on your special day.

Is it OK to ask, "What's your date of birth?"
✗ No. Your date of birth is personal information. You write it on forms in banks and hospitals.
   But you don't tell friends, classmates, or coworkers. Say, "I'm sorry. It's personal."

CHECK YOUR UNDERSTANDING

Check [✓] if it is OK to ask each question of each person.

It's OK to ask . . .	a classmate	a child	a friend
How old are you?			
When is your birthday?			
What's your date of birth?			

12 Write about your family

 ## STUDY THE MODEL

Read about Min's family.

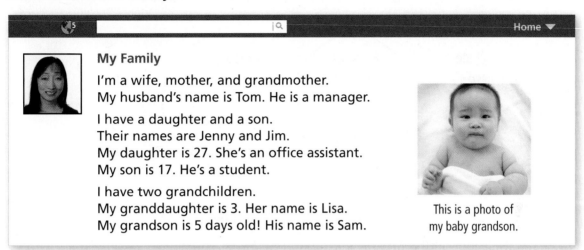

My Family

I'm a wife, mother, and grandmother.
My husband's name is Tom. He is a manager.

I have a daughter and a son.
Their names are Jenny and Jim.
My daughter is 27. She's an office assistant.
My son is 17. He's a student.

I have two grandchildren.
My granddaughter is 3. Her name is Lisa.
My grandson is 5 days old! His name is Sam.

This is a photo of
my baby grandson.

 ## CHECK YOUR UNDERSTANDING

Complete the chart.

Family member	Name	Age	Occupation
husband	Tom		manager
	Jenny		
	Jim		
	Lisa		
	Sam		

 ## BEFORE YOU WRITE

Think about your family. Complete the chart.

Family member	Name	Age	Occupation

 ## WRITE

**Write sentences about your family. Look at the model and your chart.
Write the sentences on a separate piece of paper.**

GRAMMAR

See page 147 for your Grammar Review.

VOCABULARY See page 156 for the Unit 3 Vocabulary.

Write words for each group. Tell your partner your words.

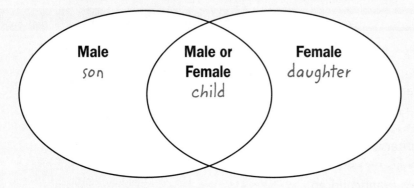

Male
son

Male or
Female
child

Female
daughter

SPELLING See page 156 for the Unit 3 Vocabulary.

CLASS Choose 10 words for a spelling test.

LISTENING PLUS

 CLASS Watch each video.
Write the story of Min's day on a separate piece of paper.

> Min gets a phone call.

B PAIRS Choose one of these conversations.
Role play the conversation for the class.

Talk about family members. (See page 35.)

Describe feelings. (See page 38.)

Talk about today's date. (See page 41.)

NOW I CAN

PAIRS See page 33 for the Unit 3 Goals. Check ☑ the things you can do.
Underline the things you want to study more. Tell your partner.

> I can _____. I need more practice with _____.

4 Ana's Good Idea

MY GOALS

Learn About:

- ☐ Clothing
- ☐ U.S. coins
- ☐ U.S. bills
- ☐ Asking about prices
- ☐ Colors and sizes
- ☐ Ordering online
- ☐ Locations at work
- ☐ Problems with clothing

Go to MyEnglishLab for more practice after each lesson.

Ana Sánchez

Ana   *Today*
We need new uniforms at the restaurant.

Talk about clothing

GET READY TO WATCH

Look at the picture. What do you think?
Ana is looking at her jacket. Why?

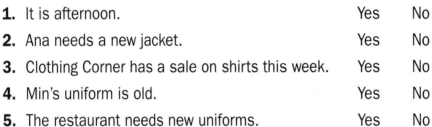

WATCH

A 📼◀ **Watch the video. Circle Yes or No.**

1.	It is afternoon.	Yes	No
2.	Ana needs a new jacket.	Yes	No
3.	Clothing Corner has a sale on shirts this week.	Yes	No
4.	Min's uniform is old.	Yes	No
5.	The restaurant needs new uniforms.	Yes	No

B 📼◀ **Watch the video again. Circle the answer.**

1. What does Min say when her uniform rips?
   a. Oh, no!   **b.** Really?   **c.** Good morning.

2. Ana asks, "What's the matter?" This means _____
   a. What are you doing?   **b.** What's wrong?

CONVERSATION

A ◀)) **Listen and read. Listen and repeat.**

Ana: I need a new jacket.

Min: Clothing Corner has a great sale on jackets this week.

B **PAIRS Practice the conversation.**

C **PAIRS Practice the conversation again.**
Talk about different clothing.

A: I need a new _____.
                          ★

B: Clothing Corner has a great sale on _____ this week.
                                                ★

> **Pronunciation Note**
>
> ◀)) **Listen and repeat.**
>
> | /s/ | /z/ | /ɪz/ |
> |---|---|---|
> | jackets | uniforms | dresses |

WHAT ABOUT YOU?

PAIRS Ask and answer: Do you buy clothes on sale? What do you buy?

Do you buy clothes on sale?

Yes. I buy coats on sale.

PRACTICAL SKILLS

U.S. coins

COINS

A 🔊 **Listen and point. Listen and repeat.**

a. a penny 1¢   **b.** a nickel 5¢   **c.** a dime 10¢   **d.** a quarter 25¢

B **Write the amount.**   (27¢   ~~40¢~~   16¢   30¢)

1. ___40¢___

2. _____

3. _____

4. _____

C 🔊 **Listen and check your answers.**

D **Write.**

1. __2__ quarters + 2 dimes = 70¢
2. ____ quarters + 1 dime + 1 nickel = 90¢
3. ____ dimes + 1 nickel + 2 pennies = 87¢
4. ____ nickels + 3 pennies = 18¢
5. 1 quarter + ____ nickels + 1 penny = 36¢
6. 2 quarters + 1 dime + ____ pennies = 67¢

> **Language Note**
> 1 penn**y**   2 penn**ies**

WHAT ABOUT YOU?

PAIRS How much change do you have? Take out your coins and count them. Tell your partner.

I have 85¢.

I'm sorry. How much?

85¢.

> **Speaking Note**
> To ask someone to repeat an amount, you can say:
> *I'm sorry. How much?*

3

U.S. bills and prices

BILLS

A ◀)) **Listen and point. Listen and repeat.**

a. One dollar $1.00

b. Five dollars $5.00

c. Ten dollars $10.00

d. Twenty dollars $20.00

B ◀)) **Listen and circle.**

1. $10.25 $10.75

2. $18.50 $80.50

3. $15.99 $50.99

4. $33.17 $33.70

5. $16.99 $69.99

6. $19.75 $90.75

> **Speaking Note**
>
> **$8.60**
> You can say *eight dollars and sixty cents*
> or *eight sixty*.

C **PAIRS** **Student A:** Say a price. **Student B:** Write the price.

WHAT DO YOU THINK?

PAIRS Which price is better? Circle *a* or *b*. Tell your partner.

1.

a. Buy one get one free

b. 2 for $10.00

2.

a. 2 for $40

b. Buy one get one 50% off

3.

a. 3 for $15.00

b. Buy 2 get 1 free

Ask about prices

GET READY TO WATCH

Ana and Victor are shopping online.
Do you shop online?

WATCH

A 🎬◀ **Watch the video. Circle the word. Write the word.**

1. Ana and Victor are talking about _____.
   <small>shoes / uniforms</small>

2. Victor asks about the _____ at Work Warehouse.
   <small>prices / hours</small>

3. Uniforms are _____ at Work Warehouse.
   <small>expensive / on sale</small>

B 🎬◀ **Watch the video again. Who says it? Circle the answer.**

1. We need new uniforms.   **a.** Victor   **b.** Ana

2. Uniforms are expensive.   **a.** Victor   **b.** Ana

3. That's a good price!   **a.** Victor   **b.** Ana

4. I'll go to Work Warehouse today.   **a.** Victor   **b.** Ana

CONVERSATION

A ◀)) **Listen and read. Listen and repeat.**

Victor: How much is the shirt?

Ana: It's $9.99

Victor: How much are the pants?

Ana: They're $14.00.

B PAIRS **Practice the conversation.**

C PAIRS **Practice the conversation again. Talk about different clothing.**

A: How much is the _____?
                        ★
B: It's $_____

A: How much are the _____?
                         ★★
B: They're $_____.

WHAT ABOUT YOU?

> Do you buy clothing in stores?
>
> Yes.

PAIRS **Ask and answer:**

Do you buy clothing in stores? Do you buy clothing online?

What's your favorite clothing store? Favorite website?

5

Questions with *How much*

STUDY *How much*

| How much **is** the shirt? | It's $9.00. |
| How much **are** the pants? | They're $14.00. |

PRACTICE

A Write *is* or *are*.

1. How much ___are___ the pants?
2. How much _____ the socks?
3. How much _____ the shirt?

4. How much _____ the sweater?
5. How much _____ the skirts?
6. How much _____ the uniform?

B ◀))) **Listen and check your answers.**

C Write.

1. **A:** _How much are_ the shoes?
   B: The shoes are $43.

2. **A:** _____ the apron?
   B: The apron is $3.00.

3. **A:** _____ the jackets?
   B: The jackets are $25.00.

4. **A:** _____?
   B: The dress is $59.00.

5. **A:** _____?
   B: The aprons are $15.00.

6. **A:** _____?
   B: The sweater is $63.00.

D ◀))) **Listen and check your answers.**

PUT IT TOGETHER

How much is the shirt?

It's $30.

PAIRS

Student A: Cover Student B's information. Ask about the prices.

Student B: Cover Student A's information. Ask about the prices.

Student A	
1. Shirt	$30.00
2. Jacket	
3. Dress	$19.00
4. Sweater	
5. Shoes	$50.00
6. Socks	
7. Pants	$19.00

Student B	
1. Shirt	$30.00
2. Jacket	$60.00
3. Dress	
4. Sweater	$17.00
5. Shoes	
6. Socks	$13.00
7. Pants	

Identify colors and sizes

 COLORS

Write.

> **Colors:** gray   green   orange   purple   ~~red~~   white
> **Clothing:** apron   dress   coat   ~~shirt~~   sweater   shirt

1. <u>a red shirt</u>

2. _____

3. _____

4. _____

5. _____

6. _____

SIZES

A ◀⟩) **Listen and point. Listen and repeat.**

1. small   **2.** medium   **3.** large   **4.** extra large

B ◀⟩) **Listen. Write the color. Listen again. Circle the size.**

	Color	Size			Color	Size
1.	black	Ⓢ M L XL	**4.**		S M L XL
2.		S M L XL	**5.**		S M L XL
3.		S M L XL	**6.**		S M L XL

PUT IT TOGETHER

PAIRS Look around the room.
Describe a classmate's clothing.
Your partner says the name.

She has a white shirt and blue pants.

That's Sofia!

PRACTICAL SKILLS

Order online

ONLINE ORDERS

A **Look at the website shopping cart. What does the website sell?**

CLOTHING WORLD

HOME   SHOP MORE

🛒 **Shopping Cart:**
5 items

Item	Details		Cost
jacket #368C	Color	red	
	Size	L	
	Price	$15.00	
	Quantity	1	$15.00
shirt #223L	Color	white	
	Size	S	
	Price	$12.00	
	Quantity	3	$36.00
skirt #320L	Color	purple	
	Size	M	
	Price	$17.00	
	Quantity	1	$17.00
		TOTAL	**$68.00**

READY TO CHECK OUT

B **Answer the questions.**

1. What is the item number for the red jacket? _368C_

2. What is the price for one white shirt? _____

3. How many white shirts are in the order? _____

4. What color is the skirt? _____

5. What is the total price of the order? _____

C **Look at the clothing. Fill in the order form.**

Item	Color	Size	Price	Quantity	Cost
Uniform PR0086			$	1	$
Apron JY0230			$	3	$27.00
				TOTAL	$

Uniform
$49.00
size — M
color — green

Apron
$9.00
size — S
color — orange

WHAT ABOUT YOU?

PAIRS **Ask and answer:** What things do you order online?

☐ clothes   ☐ medicine
☐ food   ☐ books

What things do you order online?

I order order books for school.

GET READY TO WATCH

Look at the picture.
What is Ana showing Luka?

WATCH

A ▪◀ **Watch the video. Match.**

1. Luka and Ana are   a. in the office.
2. The uniforms are   b. in the kitchen.
3. Min and Marie are   c. in the break room.
4. Victor is   d. in the storage room.

B ▪◀ **Watch the video again. Circle the answer.**

1. Ana says, "How do you like it?" Luka says, "_____"

   a. It's nice!   b. Yes, I do!

2. Ana says, "Where is everyone?" She means, "_____"

   a. Where is Victor?   b. Where are Victor, Min, and Marie?

CONVERSATION

A ◀)) **Listen and read. Listen and repeat.**

Ana: Where's my father?

Luka: He's in the office.

Ana: Where are Marie and Min?

Luka: They're in the storage room.

B PAIRS **Practice the conversation.**

C PAIRS **Practice the conversation again. Use different locations.**

A: Where's my father?

B: He's in the _____.
                  ★

A: Where are Marie and Min?

B: They're in the _____.
                     ★

WHAT DO YOU THINK?

▪◀ PAIRS Watch the video again.
Do Luka, Min, and Marie all get new uniforms?
Explain your answer.

I think . . .

STUDY Questions with *Where*

Where are you?	**I'm** in the kitchen.
Where is she?	**She's** in the living room.
Where is Victor?	**He's** in the office.
Where are Marie and Min?	**They're** in the dining room.

PRACTICE

A Match.

1. Where's
2. Where are
3. Where
4. Where are your

a. Tom and Jen?
b. is Alan?
c. sisters?
d. Ana?

B Write.

1. **A:** _Where are_ Liz and Will?
   B: They're in the _kitchen_.

2. **A:** _____ Stan?
   B: He's in the _____.

3. **A:** _____ Tina?
   B: She's in the _____.

4. **A:** _____ Pam and Sam?
   B: They're in the _____.

C ◀⟩⟩ **Listen and check your answers.**

PUT IT TOGETHER

PAIRS Ask and answer more questions about people in the picture.

Where is Scott?

He's in the kitchen.

LISTENING AND SPEAKING

Talk about problems with clothing

GET READY TO WATCH

Marie has a problem with her new uniform.
What is it?

WATCH

A 📺◀ **Watch the video. Circle *Yes* or *No*.**

1. Ana's shirt is too small.   Yes   No
2. Marie's shirt is too big.   Yes   No
3. Ana's pants are too short.   Yes   No
4. Marie's pants are too long.   Yes   No
5. Marie's apron is too small.   Yes   No
6. Ana can return the clothing.   Yes   No

B 📺◀ **Watch the video again. Circle the answer.**

Marie asks, "Can you return them?" She means, "_____"

a. Can you take the uniforms back to the store?

b. Can you buy new uniforms?

CONVERSATION

A 🔊 **Listen and read. Listen and repeat.**

Ana: What's the matter?

Marie: The shirt is too big, and the pants are too short.

Ana: I see.

B **PAIRS** **Practice the conversation.**

C **PAIRS** **Practice the conversation again. Talk about different problems.**

A: What's the matter?

B: The shirt is _____, and the pants are _____.
                         ★   ★★

A: I see.

WHAT ABOUT YOU?

GROUPS Take a survey. Ask the question.
Record the answers.

> Do you return clothing
> to stores?

> Yes. But . . .

	Yes	No	Sometimes
Do you return clothing to stores?			

11 Dress codes

GET READY

What clothing do you wear to work? What clothing do you wear to school?

READ

🔊 **Listen and read the article. What is a dress code?**

Workplace Dress Codes

Different workplaces have different dress codes. Dress codes are rules about what to wear.

Business

Men wear a suit and tie. Women wear a suit or a dress. People wear gray, blue, black, and white.

Casual

Men wear new jeans, a shirt with buttons, a belt, and shoes. Women wear a blouse with a skirt or pants, nice jeans, and nice sandals or shoes.

Business Casual

Men wear pants with a jacket. Women wear a blouse with nice pants or a skirt. People wear more colors.

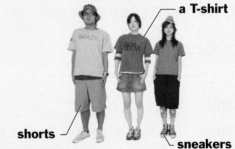

Street Wear

Men and women wear T-shirts, shorts, old jeans, sandals, and sneakers.

CHECK YOUR UNDERSTANDING

Read again. For each dress code, cross out clothing that does not belong.

Business		Business Casual		Street Wear	
suit	jacket	suit	jacket	suit	jacket
pants	tie	pants	tie	pants	tie
~~jeans~~	sneakers	jeans	sneakers	jeans	sneakers
T-shirt	sandals	T-shirt	sandals	T-shirt	sandals

Describe what you wear

 STUDY THE MODEL

Read the question and Ana's answer.

What to Wear | **What clothing do you wear at work, school, and home?**

AnaS
I work in a restaurant. At work I wear pants, a blouse, a jacket, and good shoes. Sometimes I wear a skirt or a dress.
At home I wear old jeans, a T-shirt, and sneakers.
At school I wear new jeans, a blouse, a sweater, and nice shoes.

 CHECK YOUR UNDERSTANDING

Complete the chart with Ana's information.

At Work	At School	At Home
pants		

 BEFORE YOU WRITE

What do you wear at work, school, and home? Complete the chart.

At Work	At School	At Home

WRITE

Write about what you wear at work, school, and home. Look at the model and the chart. Then copy the sentences on a separate piece of paper.

At work I wear _____.

At school I wear _____.

At home I wear _____.

GRAMMAR

See page 148 for your Grammar Review.

VOCABULARY See page 156 for the Unit 4 Vocabulary.

Write words for each group. Tell your partner your words.

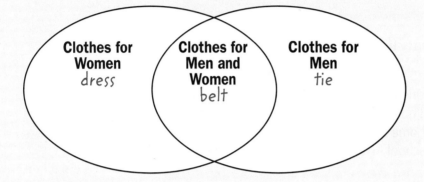

Clothes for Women
dress

Clothes for Men and Women
belt

Clothes for Men
tie

SPELLING See page 156 for the Unit 4 Vocabulary.

CLASS Choose 10 words for a spelling test.

LISTENING PLUS

 CLASS Watch each video.
Write the story of Ana's day on a separate piece of paper.

> *The restaurant needs new uniforms.*

B PAIRS Choose one of these conversations.
Role play the conversation for the class.

Ask about prices. (See page 51.)

Ask about locations at work. (See page 55.)

Talk about problems with clothing. (See page 57.)

NOW I CAN

PAIRS See page 47 for the Unit 4 Goals. Check ☑ the things you can do.
Underline the things you want to study more. Tell your partner.

> I can _____. I need more practice with _____.

5 Victor's Neighborhood Restaurant

MY GOALS

Learn About:

- ☐ Household problems
- ☐ Safety signs
- ☐ Bills
- ☐ Writing a check
- ☐ Addressing an envelope
- ☐ Places in the neighborhood
- ☐ Post office items
- ☐ Asking for and giving directions

Go to MyEnglishLab for more practice after each lesson.

Victor Sánchez

Victor　　　*Today*
Lakeside Café is a great restaurant, and it's in a nice neighborhood.

LISTENING AND SPEAKING

Identify household problems

 GET READY TO WATCH

Look at the picture. Luka has a problem.
Guess. What is it?

 WATCH

A ◼◀ **Watch the video.**
Was your guess correct?

B ◼◀ **Watch the video again. Circle *Yes* or *No*.**

1. The stove is broken.	Yes	No
2. Victor fixes the dishwasher.	Yes	No
3. Luka fixes the dishwasher.	Yes	No
4. Luka calls the repair service.	Yes	No
5. The dishwasher is out of order.	Yes	No

 CONVERSATION

A ◀))) **Listen and read. Listen and repeat.**

Luka: Call the repair service.

Victor: Why?

Luka: The dishwasher is broken!

B **PAIRS Practice the conversation.**

C **PAIRS Practice the conversation again. Talk about other appliances.**

A: Call the repair service!

B: Why?

A: The _____ is broken!
         ★

WHAT ABOUT YOU?

GROUPS Ask and answer: What appliances do you have at work?
What appliances do you have at home?

At work	At home	
☐	☐	refrigerator
☐	☐	dishwasher
☐	☐	microwave
☐	☐	washing machine
☐	☐	dryer
☐	☐	stove

What appliances do you have at work?

We have two refrigerators and a stove . . .

2 The imperative

STUDY The imperative

> **Grammar Note**
> Use the imperative to give directions.

Open the door. **Don't open the door.**

PRACTICE

A Circle the word. Write the word.

1. ___Open___ the door.
   Put / (Open)

2. _____ the door.
   Close / Turn on

3. _____ the button.
   Press / Don't Press

4. _____ the power.
   Call / Turn off

5. _____ the clothes
   Put / Press
   in the washing machine.

6. _____ the repair
   Open / Call
   service.

B 🔊 Listen and check your answers.

C Write the missing sentences.

✓	🚫
Open the door.	Don't open the door.
	Don't put the clothes in the washing machine.
Put the food in the microwave.	
Close the door.	
	Don't turn off the power.

PUT IT TOGETHER

> Open the door.

PAIRS Choose sentences from Exercise C.
Read them to your partner. Act out your partner's directions.

SAFETY SIGNS

A ◄))) **Listen and point. Listen and repeat.**

a.

b.

c.

d.

e.

f.

B **Read. Write the letter of the sign.**

1. _e_ You can't go in that room.

2. ____ You can't smoke in this workplace.

3. ____ Watch out—there's water on the floor.

4. ____ The refrigerator is broken.

C ◄))) **Listen. Write the letter of the sign.**

1. ____   **4.** ____

2. ____   **5.** ____

3. ____   **6.** ____

WHAT ABOUT YOU?

GROUPS **Ask and answer:** Where do you see safety signs?

> Where do you see safety signs?

> I see "No Smoking" signs in restaurants.

LISTENING AND SPEAKING

Talk about bills

 GET READY TO WATCH

Ana and Victor are talking about bills.
What bills do you get?

 WATCH

A 🎥 **Watch the video. Check [✓] the bills that Ana and Victor talk about.**

☐ water bill   ☐ rent bill

☐ gas bill   ☐ electric bill

☐ phone bill   ☐ Internet bill

☐ repair bill

B **Match.**

1. repair bill   **a.** $750

2. gas bill   **b.** $250

3. electric bill   **c.** $600

C 🎥 **Watch the video again. Circle the answer.**

What does Ana say when she sees the bills?

a. Wow!   **b.** Oh.

 CONVERSATION

A 🔊 **Listen and read. Listen and repeat.**

Victor: How much is the gas bill?

Ana: It's six hundred dollars.

B **PAIRS Practice the conversation.**

C **PAIRS Practice the conversation again. Talk about other types of bills.**

A: How much is the _____ bill?
★

B: It's _____.
★★

Speaking Note	
🔊 **Listen and repeat.**	
100	one hundred
150	one hundred fifty
200	two hundred
1,000	one thousand
1,150	one thousand, one hundred fifty

WHAT ABOUT YOU?

GROUPS Ask and answer: How do you get your bills?

☐ in the mail

☐ by email

How do you get your bills?

I get my Internet bill by email.

PRACTICAL SKILLS

Write a check

 ### READ A CHECK

Look at the check. Match the questions and answers.

1. Who is the check from? ——— 10/14/15
2. Who is the check to? Jones Appliance Repair
3. What is the date on the check? Lakeside Café
4. How much money is the check for? 4402
5. What is the account number? $250.00

 ### WRITE A CHECK

Complete the check. See page 160 for a list of numbers.
Use this information:

The check is to the City of Chicago. The amount is $300.00. Water account: #102379

WHAT ABOUT YOU?

PAIRS Ask and answer: Do you use checks? What do you use them for?

Do you use checks?

Yes. I use checks for my bills.

PRACTICAL SKILLS

Address an envelope

READ AND WRITE AN ADDRESS

A **Read. Write the words on the lines.**

~~Name of person~~	Address	Zip Code
Name of business	State	City

Lakeside Café
5305 North Clark St.
Chicago, IL 60640

1. _Name of person_ ——•Joe Jones

Jones Appliance Repair •—— 2. _____

3. _____ •12019 Lake Shore Dr.

Barrington, IL 60010 •—— 6. _____

4. _____

5. _____

B **Address this envelope from you to your teacher.**

_____
_____
_____

_____
_____
_____
_____

WHAT ABOUT YOU?

PAIRS Ask and answer: What's your address?

What's your address?

24 Juniper Street.

Could you spell *Juniper*, please?

J-U-N-I-P-E-R.

Speaking Note

To help you understand, you can ask someone to spell a word.

7

Talk about places in the neighborhood

GET READY TO WATCH

Marie has checks to mail.
Where do you go to mail things?

WATCH

A ▬◀ **Watch the video. Circle *Yes* or *No*.**

1. Marie is going to the supermarket.	Yes	No
2. Marie is new to the neighborhood.	Yes	No
3. The post office and the library are on First Street.	Yes	No
4. The park is on West State Street.	Yes	No

B ▬◀ **Watch the video again. Circle the answer.**

1. When Victor says, "Thank you," Marie says, "_____"

   a. Sure!   **b.** You're welcome.   **c.** Oh!

2. How does Marie say goodbye?

   a. I'll be back soon.   **b.** You're welcome.   **c.** Oh, right!

CONVERSATION

A ◀))) **Listen and read. Listen and repeat.**

Marie: Where's the post office?

Victor: It's on West State Street.

B **PAIRS Practice the conversation.**

C **PAIRS Practice the conversation again. Talk about other places.**

A: Where's the _____?
          ★

B: It's on West State Street.

ROLE PLAY

PAIRS Ask about places in the neighborhood near your school.
Use real street names.

Where's the hospital?

It's on Walnut Street.

GRAMMAR

Prepositions of location

STUDY Prepositions of location

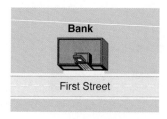

on

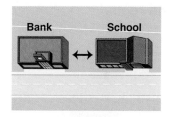

next to

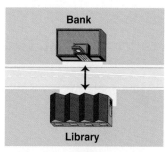

across from

The bank is **on** First Street.

The bank is **next to** the school.

The bank is **across from** the library.

PRACTICE

A **Look at the map. Write *on*, *next to*, or *across from*.**

1. The supermarket is ____next to____ the park.

2. The library is _____ the supermarket.

3. The bank is _____ the post office.

4. The pharmacy is _____ Main Street.

5. The hospital is _____ the bank.

B ◀)) **Listen and check your answers.**

PUT IT TOGETHER

PAIRS Ask and answer more questions about the places on the map.

> Where's the supermarket?

> The supermarket is on Main Street.
> It's across from the library.

THE POST OFFICE

 A ◀))) **Listen and point. Listen and repeat.**

1. a stamp   **2.** an envelope   **3.** a money order

4. a package   **5.** a post office box

 B ◀))) **Listen and circle.**

1. a package	a stamp	**4.** a package	a stamp
2. a money order	a stamp	**5.** a package	an envelope
3. a post office box	an envelope	**6.** a money order	stamps

C **Write.**

(a stamp   a post office box   a money order)

1. You want to send money home. You go to the post office.

You ask for _____.

2. You need a place to get mail. You go to the post office.

You ask for _____.

3. You want to send a letter. You go to the post office.

You ask for _____.

WHAT ABOUT YOU?

GROUPS **Ask and answer:** What do you get at the ____?

What do you get at
the post office?

I get stamps.

post office
bank
library
supermarket

10

Ask for and give directions

GET READY TO WATCH

Victor is giving directions.
When do you ask for directions?

WATCH

◼◀ **Watch the video. Match.**

1. The customers like   **a.** a pharmacy.
2. They ask for directions to   **b.** West Elm Street.
3. The pharmacy is on   **c.** the restaurant.
4. Victor gives   **d.** directions.

CONVERSATION

A ◀ᐣ) **Listen and read. Listen and repeat.**

Customer: Is there a pharmacy near here?

Victor: Yes. Go straight one block. Then turn right. It's on West Elm Street.

Customer: Thank you.

B **PAIRS** **Practice the conversation.**

C **PAIRS** **Practice the conversation again. Use new places and new directions.**

A: Is there a ____ near here?

B: Yes. Go straight ____ ____. Then turn ____. It's on ____.

A: Thank you.

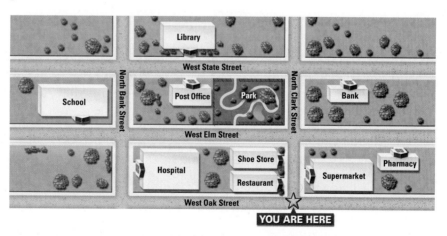

ROLE PLAY

PAIRS Look at Exercise C.
Ask for and give more directions.

Is there a bank near here?

Yes. Go two blocks. Then turn right.

11

Saving money at the supermarket

GET READY

Do you like to shop for food?

READ

◀)) **Listen and read the article. What is the article about?**

www.savingmoney.com

$AVING MONEY | At the Supermarket | HOME | COUPONS | SPECIAL OFFERS | ABOUT US | CONTACT US

Shopping Tips

Eat before you shop.
Don't go to the supermarket hungry. Hungry shoppers buy more.

Write a shopping list.
Look in your kitchen. Open your refrigerator. What is in your refrigerator? What do you need? Write the foods you need.

Buy store brands.
Brand names are more expensive. Store brands are not so expensive. The name is different. The price is different. But sometimes the food is the same!

Look carefully at sale prices.
Sometimes sale prices are very good. Sometimes sale prices are not good. Look at the sale price and look at the regular price. What's the difference?

Use coupons.
Look for coupons online or in the mail. Be careful! Sometimes coupons are for more expensive foods.

CHECK YOUR UNDERSTANDING

A **Read the article again. Check [✓] Do or Don't.**

	Do	Don't	
1.	☐	☐	Go to the supermarket hungry.
2.	☐	☐	Buy brand-name foods.
3.	☐	☐	Look at the sale price and regular price.
4.	☐	☐	Use coupons.
5.	☐	☐	Write a list of foods you need.

B **GROUPS Which tip is best? Tell your classmates.**

12 Write about your neighborhood

 ## STUDY THE MODEL

Read the website for Lakeside Café.

www.lakesidecafe.com

Lakeside Café

MENU
RESERVATIONS
CONTACT US
DIRECTIONS

Come to our restaurant!
We are in the Andersonville neighborhood.
It's a nice neighborhood.
Our restaurant is on North Clark Street.
It is near a park and a bank.
It is next to a shoe store.
It is across from a supermarket.

 ## CHECK YOUR UNDERSTANDING

Look back at the website. Complete the map.

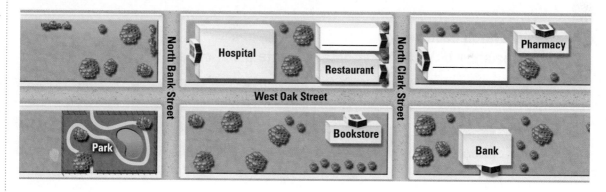

North Bank Street

Hospital

Restaurant

West Oak Street

North Clark Street

Pharmacy

Park

Bookstore

Bank

 ## BEFORE YOU WRITE

Think about your home and neighborhood.
Draw a map of your street and neighborhood on a separate piece of paper.

 ## WRITE

Describe your street and neighborhood. Look at the model and your map.
Then copy the sentences on a separate piece of paper.

I am in the _____ neighborhood.

I am on _____ street.

My home is next to _____.

My home is across from _____.

My home is near _____.

GRAMMAR

See page 149 for your Grammar Review.

VOCABULARY See page 157 for the Unit 5 Vocabulary.

Find the word that is different.

1. stamp	road	post office box	money order
2. rent	library	park	post office
3. state	zip code	city	Internet
4. boulevard	check	avenue	street
5. stove	bill	microwave	refrigerator
6. water	electricity	block	gas
7. left	address	straight	right
8. bank	hundred	fifty	thousand

SPELLING See page 157 for the Unit 5 Vocabulary.

CLASS Choose 10 words for a spelling test.

 ## LISTENING PLUS

A CLASS Watch each video.

Write the story of Victor's day on a separate piece of paper.

The dishwasher is broken. Victor calls the repairman.

B PAIRS Choose one of these conversations.

Role play the conversation for the class.

Talk about bills. (See page 65.)

Talk about places in the neighborhood. (See page 68.)

Ask for and give directions. (See page 71.)

NOW I CAN

PAIRS See page 61 for the Unit 5 Goals. Check ☑ the things you can do.
Underline the things you want to study more. Tell your partner.

I can ____. I need more practice with ____.

6 Marie's Customers

Marie Baptiste

Marie   *Today*
I like my job. I try new foods every day.

PRACTICAL SKILLS

Talk about food

FOODS

A ◀))) **Listen and point. Listen and repeat.**

1. bread

2. cheese

3. chicken

4. fish

5. meat

6. milk

7. pasta

8. rice

B **Write the foods in the correct categories.**

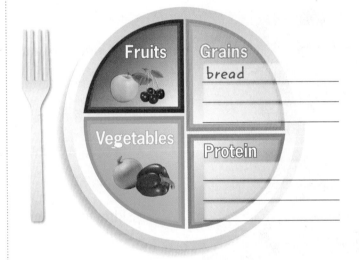

Fruits

Grains
bread
_____
_____

Vegetables

Protein
_____
_____
_____

Dairy

_____ cheese _____
_____

C ◀))) **Listen and write the foods you hear.**

1. _pasta_   3. _____   5. _____

2. _____   4. _____   6. _____

WHAT ABOUT YOU?

PAIRS Ask and answer: What foods do you eat?

I eat fish.

Me, too.

Speaking Note

To agree with someone, you can say: *Me, too* or *I do, too.*

GET READY TO WATCH

Marie doesn't like onions.
Do you like onions?

WATCH

A ■◀ **Watch the video. Circle the answer.**

1. Min asks Marie to try _____.

   a. the onion soup   **b.** the potato salad   **c.** the onion soup and the potato salad

2. Marie tries _____.

   a. the onion soup   **b.** the potato salad   **c.** the onion soup and the potato salad

3. Marie likes _____.

   a. the onion soup   **b.** the potato salad   **c.** the onion soup and the potato salad

B ■◀ **Watch the video again. Circle the answer.**

Marie says the potato salad is delicious. This means it is _____.

a. bad   **b.** good   **c.** very good

CONVERSATION

A ◀)) **Listen and read. Listen and repeat.**

Min: Do you like potatoes?

Marie: Yes. I like potatoes.

Spelling Note		
1 tomato	→	2 tomatoes
1 potato	→	4 potatoes
1 pepper	→	3 peppers

B **PAIRS** **Practice the conversation.**

C **PAIRS** **Practice the conversation 2 more times.**
First, answer *yes*. Then, answer *no*. Talk about different foods.

A: Do you like _____?
                 ★

B: Yes. I like _____.
               ★

A: Do you like _____?
                 ★

B: No. I don't like _____.
                 ★

WHAT DO YOU THINK?

■◀ **GROUPS** Watch the video again.
Min tells the servers about the
specials each day. Why?

I think . . .

3 Simple present tense

STUDY Simple present tense: *I, you, we, they*

They **like** pasta.   They **want** pasta.   Tim and Jen **need** water.   Tim and Jen **have** water.

I **like** apples. →	I **don't like** bananas.
You **have** potatoes. →	You **don't have** peppers or beans.
We **need** beef. →	We **don't need** chicken.
They **want** rice. →	They **don't want** pasta.

PRACTICE

A **Write.**

1. I ___don't like___ cheese, but I _____ milk.

    not like   *like*

2. The customers _____ salad. They _____ bread.

                      want   *not want*

3. We _____ two specials today. We _____ the rice salad.

        have   *not have*

4. You _____ onions, but you _____ tomatoes.

    not need   *need*

B ◄)) **Listen and check your answers.**

C **Circle the answer. Then write a sentence.**

1. Do you like peppers?   (Yes)   No   ___I like peppers.___
2. Do you like onions?   Yes   No   _____
3. Do you like apples?   Yes   No   _____
4. Do you like fish?   Yes   No   _____
5. Do you like tomatoes?   Yes   No   _____

WHAT ABOUT YOU?

PAIRS Write a list of foods you like.
Talk to your partner.
What foods do you both like?

> I like oranges.
>> I do, too.

PRACTICAL SKILLS

Containers and quantities

CONTAINERS AND QUANTITIES

A ◀)) **Listen and point. Listen and repeat.**

1. **a bag of carrots**   2. **a bottle of juice**   3. **a can of corn**

4. **a box of cereal**   5. **a pound of shrimp**   6. **a carton of eggs**

B ◀)) **Listen and circle.**

1. a bag of rice   a box of rice
2. four pounds of beans   four cans of beans
3. two cans of juice   two bottles of juice
4. a bag of pasta   a box of pasta
5. three pounds of fish   three cans of fish

C **PAIRS** **Write as many foods as you can in each category. Tell the class.**

apples	beans	carrots	cereal	cheese
chicken	juice	meat	onions	potatoes
rice	shrimp	tomatoes		

A Bag of	A Bottle of	A Can of	A Box of	A Pound of
apples				

WHAT ABOUT YOU?

PAIRS Look at the chart in Exercise C. Make a grocery list. Tell your partner what foods you need.

> I need two boxes of cereal, a bag of potatoes . . .

5

Read a menu

A MENU

 A ◀))) **Listen and point. Listen and repeat.**

Lakeside Café

1 **Sandwiches**
2 Fish sandwich
3 Egg sandwich
4 Cheese sandwich

5 **Soup**
6 Vegetable
7 Tomato

8 **Drinks**
9 Fruit juice   12 Tea
10 Milk   13 Coffee
11 Iced tea   14 Soda

15 **Salads**
16 Chicken salad
17 Rice salad
18 Pasta salad
19 Green salad

20 **Dessert**
21 Fruit salad
22 Apple pie

B ◀))) **Listen and circle.**

1. cheese sandwich   chicken salad   coffee   tea

2. egg sandwich   fish sandwich   milk   fruit juice

3. pasta salad   rice salad   coffee   tea

4. potato soup   tomato soup   milk   juice

C **PAIRS Look at the menu. Which foods do you like? Make a list.
Tell your partner.**

WHAT ABOUT YOU?

PAIRS Ask and answer: What's your favorite restaurant?
What do you order there?

What's your favorite restaurant?

My favorite restaurant is . . .

Order food in a restaurant

 GET READY TO WATCH

The customers are ordering lunch.
What do you eat for lunch?

 WATCH

A ◼◀ **Watch the video.**
Check [✓] the foods the customers order.

☐ potato salad   ☐ a green salad   ☐ orange juice

☐ a cheese sandwich   ☐ vegetable soup   ☐ iced tea

☐ a chicken sandwich   ☐ onion soup   ☐ water

B ◼◀ **Watch the video again. Circle the answer.**

Marie asks, "Anything else?" She means, "____"

a. Would you like to order more food?

b. Are you ready to order?

c. Would you like something to drink?

CONVERSATION

A ◀)) **Listen and read. Listen and repeat.**

Marie: Are you ready to order?

Customer: Yes. I'd like a cheese sandwich.

Marie: OK. Anything to drink?

Customer: Yes. Iced tea, please.

> **Speaking Note**
>
> **I'd like** and **I like** are different.
> *I'd like soup.* = I want soup.
> *I like soup.* = Soup is good, but I don't
>   want soup now.

B **PAIRS** Practice the conversation.

C **PAIRS** Practice the conversation again. Use different foods.

A: Are you ready to order?

B: Yes. I'd like a _____.
                      ★

A: OK. Anything to drink?

B: Yes. _____, please.
           ★★

ROLE PLAY

GROUPS Order more food from the menu in Lesson 5.

> I'd like vegetable soup
> and a cheese sandwich.

7

Make and respond to a complaint

GET READY TO WATCH

Marie's customer makes a complaint.
She doesn't like the food. Guess.
What does Marie do?

WATCH

A 📹 **Watch the video.**
Was your guess correct?

B 📹 **Watch the video again. Circle Yes or No.**

1. The customer likes the vegetable soup.	Yes	No
2. The pasta salad has peppers.	Yes	No
3. The onion soup has peppers.	Yes	No
4. The customer orders onion soup.	Yes	No

CONVERSATION

A 🔊 **Listen and read. Listen and repeat.**

Customer: We have a small problem.

Marie: What's wrong?

Customer: The soup has peppers. My daughter doesn't like peppers.

Marie: Oh, I'm sorry.

B **PAIRS Practice the conversation.**

C **PAIRS Practice the conversation again. Talk about different foods.**

A: We have a small problem.

B: What's wrong?

A: The _____ has _____. My daughter doesn't
　　　　★　　　　　　★★
like _____.
　　　★★

B: Oh, I'm sorry.

WHAT DO YOU THINK?

PAIRS Some people say: "The customer is always right."
What do you think it means? Do you agree?

> I think . . .

GRAMMAR

Simple present tense

STUDY Simple present tense: *She, he, it*

She **likes** chicken.	She **doesn't like** fish.
He **needs** water.	He **doesn't need** juice.
Marie **wants** an apple.	She **doesn't want** a banana.
It **has** peppers.	It **doesn't have** tomatoes.

Grammar Note

I **have**	She **has**
You **have**	He **has**
We **have**	It **has**
They **have**	

PRACTICE

A **Write.**

1. Marie _____*likes*_____ shrimp. She _____ fish.
   _{like}   _{not like}

2. The soup _____ more water, but it _____ anything else.
   _{need}   _{not need}

3. The salad _____ carrots. It _____ cucumbers.
   _{not have}   _{have}

4. The customer _____ soup, but he _____ bread.
   _{want}   _{not want}

B ◀)) **Listen and check your answers.**

C **Write.**

1. I _*don't like*_ broccoli.
   _{not like}

2. They _____ milk in their coffee.
   _{want}

3. She _____ three cans of corn.
   _{need}

4. The soup _____ shrimp.
   _{have}

5. We _____ dessert.
   _{not want}

6. You _____ eggs.
   _{not need}

7. Luka _____ onions.
   _{like}

8. Victor and Ana _____ lettuce.
   _{not have}

D ◀)) **Listen and check your answers.**

PUT IT TOGETHER

CLASS Stand in a circle. Follow the model.

Lin likes mushrooms.
Brad likes pasta.
I like shrimp.

I like mushrooms.

Lin likes mushrooms.
I like pasta.

Lin

Brad

Frank

9

Ask for and give change

GET READY TO WATCH

Look at the picture. Guess.
What does the customer want?

WATCH

A 📹◀ **Watch the video. Was your guess correct?**

B 📹◀ **Watch the video again. Put the sentences in order.**

_____ The customer pays for the meal.

_____ The customer leaves a tip.

__1__ The customer asks for the check.

_____ The customer asks for change.

a tip

C **Circle the answer.**
What does Marie say when she gives the check to the customer?

a. Here you are.

b. You want the check.

c. Please.

CONVERSATION

A 🔊))) **Listen and read. Listen and repeat.**

Customer: Do you have change for a twenty?

Marie: Yes. Here you go.

Customer: Thank you!

> **Speaking Note**
> Here you go. = Here you are.

B **PAIRS** **Practice the conversation.**

C **PAIRS** **Practice the conversation again. Use new words.**

A: Do you have change for a _____?
                                    ★

B: Yes. _____.
            ★★

A: Thank you!

WHAT DO YOU THINK?

GROUPS Marie gets a big tip. Why?

> I think . . .

PRACTICAL SKILLS

10

Methods of payment

WAYS TO PAY

A ◀))) **Listen and point. Listen and repeat.**

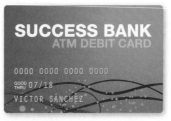

1. a credit card   **2.** a debit card   **3.** cash

4. a check   **5.** a money order

B ◀))) **Listen and circle.**

1. debit card	check	**4.** debit card	money order
2. credit card	debit card	**5.** money order	check
3. cash	check	**6.** check	cash

C **PAIRS** **Complete the sentences. Tell your partner.**

Example: In a restaurant, I pay with _____ *cash* _____.

1. In a restaurant, I pay with _____.

2. In a clothing store, I pay with _____.

3. In a supermarket, I pay with _____.

4. In a post office, I pay with _____.

5. On a website, I pay with _____.

WHAT ABOUT YOU?

GROUPS Take a survey. Ask the question. Record the answers.

	Cash	Credit card
Do you tip with cash or a credit card?		

Do you tip with cash or a credit card?

I tip with cash.

11

Tipping

GET READY

Who do you tip? How much do you tip?

READ

◀») **Quickly read the article. Who do people tip? Listen and read the article.**

A Guide to Tipping

In the U.S., customers tip food servers, hairdressers, cab drivers, and others. If the service is good, customers tip more. Here are some guidelines:

Who: A server
Where: In a restaurant
How much: Tip 10% for poor service.
Tip 15% for OK service.
Tip 20% for excellent service.

Who: A restaurant delivery person
Where: At your home
How much: Tip $2 or more.
For a big bill, tip 10%.

Who: A cab driver
Where: In a taxi
How much: Tip 10% to 20% of the bill.

Who: A hairdresser
Where: In a salon
How much: Tip 10%.

CHECK YOUR UNDERSTANDING

A **Write. Then tell the class.**

1. In a restaurant: The service is excellent. The bill is $40.

   The tip is $_____.

2. In a salon: The hairdresser does a good job. The bill is $30.

   The tip is $_____.

3. In a taxi. The service is excellent. The bill is $20.

   The tip is $_____.

4. At home: The delivery person is late. The food is cold. The bill is $50.

   The tip is $_____.

5. In a restaurant: The service is poor. The bill is $60.

   The tip is $_____.

B **GROUPS** **Ask and answer:** Who do you tip in your home country? How much?

Who do you tip in your home country?

I tip servers and cab drivers.

Write about your favorite foods

STUDY THE MODEL

Read about Marie's favorite foods.

Fast Food

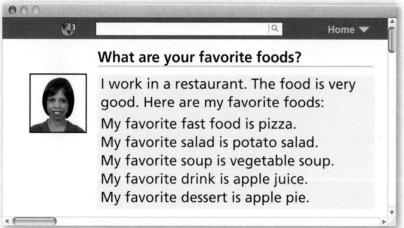

What are your favorite foods?

I work in a restaurant. The food is very good. Here are my favorite foods:
My favorite fast food is pizza.
My favorite salad is potato salad.
My favorite soup is vegetable soup.
My favorite drink is apple juice.
My favorite dessert is apple pie.

pizza

french fries

fried chicken

CHECK YOUR UNDERSTANDING

Read the model again. Complete the chart.

	Salad	Soup	Drink	Dessert	Fast food
Marie's favorite					

BEFORE YOU WRITE

Think about your favorite foods. Write your favorite foods in the chart.

	Salad	Soup	Drink	Dessert	Fast food
Your favorite					

WRITE

On a separate piece of paper, write 5 sentences about your favorite foods. Look at the model and your chart.

GRAMMAR

See page 150 for your Grammar Review.

VOCABULARY See page 157 for the Unit 6 Vocabulary.

Find words for each group. Tell a classmate your words.

Vegetables	Drinks	Containers	Ways to Pay
onions	soda	bag	a debit card

SPELLING See page 157 for the Unit 6 Vocabulary.

CLASS Choose 10 words for a spelling test.

LISTENING PLUS

A **CLASS Watch each video.**
Write the story of Marie's day on a separate piece of paper.

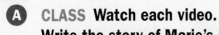

Marie tries today's specials.

B **PAIRS Choose one of these conversations.**
Role play the conversation for the class.

Order food in a restaurant. (See page 81.)

Make and respond to a complaint. (See page 82.)

Ask for and give change. (See page 84.)

NOW I CAN

PAIRS See page 75 for the Unit 6 Goals. Check ☑ the things you can do.
Underline the things you want to study more. Tell your partner.

> I can _____. I need more practice with _____.

7 Min Doesn't Feel Well

MY GOALS

Learn About:

☐ Parts of the body

☐ Common ailments

☐ Medicines

☐ Medicine labels

☐ Making an appointment

☐ Visiting the doctor

☐ Calling in sick

☐ Items in a store

Go to MyEnglishLab for more practice after each lesson.

Min Lee

Min   *Today*
I don't feel well. I have a headache and a sore throat.

1

Parts of the body

FACE AND BODY

A ◀») **Listen and point. Listen and repeat.**

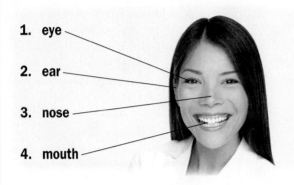

1. eye
2. ear
3. nose
4. mouth

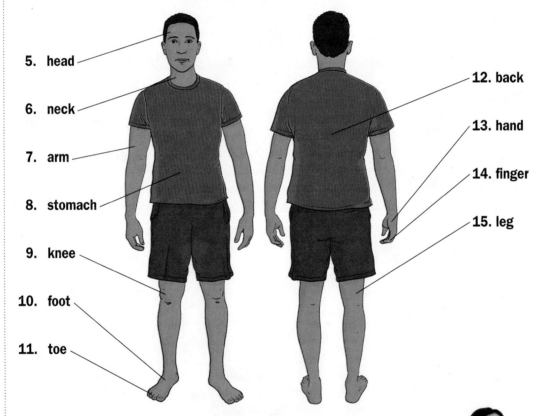

5. head
6. neck
7. arm
8. stomach
9. knee
10. foot
11. toe

12. back
13. hand
14. finger
15. leg

B ◀») **Listen and write.**

1. Her _____ hurts.
2. His _____ hurts.
3. Her _____ hurts.
4. His _____ hurts.

PUT IT TOGETHER

PAIRS **Student A:** Say a part of the body.

Student B: Point to the part of the body in the picture.

LISTENING AND SPEAKING

Talk about common ailments

GET READY TO WATCH

Min is at work. She is sick.
What do you do when you are sick at work?

WATCH

A ◼◀ **Watch the video. Check [✓] Min's ailments.**

- ☐ a headache
- ☐ a fever
- ☐ a sore throat
- ☐ a stomachache
- ☐ a runny nose
- ☐ a cough

B ◼◀ **Watch the video again. Circle the answer.**

1. Luka says, "My daughter is sick." Min says, "____"

    a. Is she at school?   **b.** Oh, I'm sorry.

2. Min says, "I don't feel well." She means, "____"

    a. I'm sick.   **b.** I'm not happy.

CONVERSATION

A ◀》) **Listen and read. Listen and repeat.**

Luka: What's the matter?

Min: I have a headache.

Luka: Do you have a sore throat?

Min: Yes, I do.

B PAIRS **Practice the conversation.**

C PAIRS **Practice the conversation again. Talk about different ailments.**

A: What's the matter?

B: I have a _____.
               ★

A: Do you have a _____?
                  ★

B: Yes, I do.

WHAT DO YOU THINK?

◼◀ GROUPS Watch the video again. What do you think?
Does Min have the flu? Why?

    I think . . .

STUDY Simple present tense: *Yes/no* questions

Questions	Answers	
Do you **have** a headache?	Yes, I **do**.	No, I **don't**.
Do they **need** medicine?	Yes, they **do**.	No, they **don't**.
Do Lisa and Sam **need** medicine?	Yes, they **do**.	No, they **don't**.

Does she **have** a headache?	Yes, she **does**.	No, she **doesn't**.
Does he **need** medicine?	Yes, he **does**.	No, he **doesn't**.
Does Min **need** medicine?	Yes, she **does**.	No, she **doesn't**.

 PRACTICE

A Write. Use *do*, *does*, *don't*, and *doesn't*.

1. **A:** _____Do_____ you have a headache?

   B: No, I _____.

2. **A:** _____ she need medicine?

   B: Yes, she _____.

3. **A:** _____ Tom have a cough?

   B: Yes, he _____.

4. **A:** _____ they want tea?

   B: Yes, they _____.

5. **A:** _____ Jack have a fever?

   B: No, he _____.

6. **A:** _____ Kim and Sammi have colds?

   B: No, they _____.

B ◀))) **Listen and check your answers.**

PUT IT TOGETHER

PAIRS **Student A:** Cover Student B's information. Ask about the ailments.
Student B: Cover Student A's information. Ask about the ailments.

Does Jim have a headache?

No, he doesn't.

Student A	Jim	Tina
headache	✗	✓
sore throat		✓
fever		✗
runny nose		✓

Student B	Jim	Tina
headache	✗	
sore throat	✓	
fever	✓	
runny nose	✗	

LISTENING AND SPEAKING

Identify medicines

GET READY TO WATCH

Min has a headache and a fever.
What medicine does she need?

WATCH

A ■◀ **Watch the video.**
Circle the answer.

1. What does Min ask for?

   a. pain medicine   **b.** allergy medicine

2. What does Ana do?

   a. She buys some medicine.   **b.** She looks for some medicine.

B ■◀ **Watch the video again. Check [✓] the directions Ana and Victor give Min.**

☐ Take this pain medicine.   ☐ Go home.

☐ Take this cough medicine.   ☐ See a doctor.

☐ Go back to work.   ☐ See your husband.

CONVERSATION

A ◀))) **Listen and read. Listen and repeat.**

Ana: Take this pain medicine. It's good for a headache and a fever.

Min: OK. Thank you.

B **PAIRS** **Practice the conversation.**

C **PAIRS** **Practice the conversation again.**
Talk about different medicines and ailments.

A: Take this _____. It's good for a _____.
                  ★   ★★

B: OK. Thank you.

WHAT ABOUT YOU?

PAIRS **Ask and answer:** What medicines do you have at home?

I have allergy medicine and ibuprofen.

I do, too. And I have . . .

STUDY Demonstratives

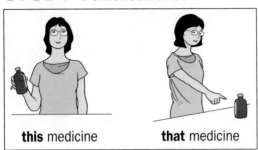

this medicine   **that** medicine

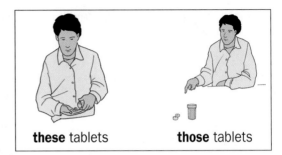

these tablets   **those** tablets

 PRACTICE

A Write *This* or *These*.

1. _____This_____ medicine is expensive!

2. _____ tablets are good for a cold.

3. _____ cough medicine is old.

4. _____ tablets are for a stomachache.

5. _____ allergy medicine is new.

6. _____ box of tablets is new.

B ◀)) Listen and check your answers.

C Write *That* or *Those*.

1. _____Those_____ tablets are for a headache.

2. _____ bottle of medicine is for a cough.

3. _____ medicine is for children.

4. _____ tablets are for my grandmother.

5. _____ cough medicine is old.

6. _____ bottles are for me.

D ◀)) Listen and check your answers.

PUT IT TOGETHER

PAIRS Point to and identify furniture in your classroom.
Use *this, that, these, those.*

this desk

those chairs

6

Read medicine labels

MEDICINE DIRECTIONS

A ◀)) **Listen and point. Listen and repeat.**

| 1. a tablespoon | 2. a teaspoon | 3. tablets | 4. every four hours | 5. twice a day |

B ◀)) **Listen and write.**

1. Take __2__ tablets every __6__ hours.
2. Take ____ tablets every ____ hours.
3. Take ____ tablespoons every ____ hours.
4. Take ____ teaspoons every ____ hours.
5. Take ____ tablet every ____ hours.

C **Read the labels. Complete the medicine schedule.**

1. Take ___2 tablespoons___ at ___6:00 A.M.___
   ___12:00 P.M.___
   _____
   _____

2. Take _____ at ___6:00 A.M.___
   _____

3. Take _____ at ___10:00 A.M.___
   _____
   _____
   _____

4. Take _____ at ___6:00 A.M.___
   _____
   _____

WHAT ABOUT YOU?

PAIRS You have some new medicine. You don't know the directions.
What do you do?

☐ I read the label. ☐ I ask at the pharmacy.

☐ I ask a friend. ☐ I call my doctor.

> I call my doctor.

Make an appointment

 GET READY TO WATCH

Look at the picture. Guess.
Who is Min calling?

WATCH

A ◼◀ **Watch the video.**
Was your guess correct?

B ◼◀ **Watch the video again.**
Check [✓] the questions the receptionist asks Min.

☐ What's the problem?   ☐ What's your address?

☐ What medicine do you take? ☐ What's your date of birth?

☐ How do you spell your name? ☐ What's your phone number?

CONVERSATION

A ◀))) **Listen and read. Listen and repeat.**

Min:	I'd like to make an appointment.
Receptionist:	What's the problem?
Min:	I have a headache and a fever.
Receptionist:	Is 1:00 OK?
Min:	Yes.

B PAIRS **Practice the conversation.**

C PAIRS **Practice the conversation again. Use different ailments and times.**

A: I'd like to make an appointment.

B: What's the problem?

A: I have a _____.
            ★

B: Is _____ OK?
        ★★

A: Yes.

WHAT ABOUT YOU?

GROUPS Take a survey. Ask the question.
Record the answers.

How do you make appointments
with your doctor?

I walk in.

	Call	Walk In	Go Online
How do you make appointments with your doctor?			

Visit the doctor

FOLLOW THE DOCTOR'S DIRECTIONS

A ◀)) **Listen and point. Listen and repeat.**

1. Take off your shoes.

2. Stand on the scale.

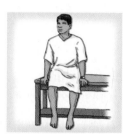

3. Sit on the table.

4. Breathe in.

5. Breathe out.

6. Lie down.

7. Open your mouth.

8. Roll up your sleeve.

9. Look straight ahead.

B ◀)) **Listen. Number the directions *1, 2, 3*.**

Conversation 1	Conversation 2	Conversation 3
____ Open your mouth.	____ Stand on the scale.	____ Lie down.
____ Breath out.	____ Take off your shoes.	____ Take off your shoes.
_1_ Breath in.	____ Sit on the table.	____ Sit on the table.

PUT IT TOGETHER

PAIRS **Student A:** Give your partner directions.
Student B: Follow the directions.

Breathe in.

Could you repeat that, please?

Breathe in.

> **Speaking Note**
>
> To ask someone to repeat, you can say:
> *Can you repeat that please?*

LISTENING AND SPEAKING

9 Call in sick

 GET READY TO WATCH

Min is calling in sick.

Guess. What does she say?

 WATCH

A ■◀ **Watch the video.**
Was your guess correct?

B ■◀ **Watch the video again. Circle *Yes* or *No*.**

1. Victor calls Min.   Yes   No

2. Min has a stomachache.   Yes   No

3. Min can come to work.   Yes   No

CONVERSATION

A ◀)) **Listen and read. Listen and repeat.**

Min: I have the flu.

Victor: I'm sorry to hear that. You should drink tea. And rest.

Min: OK. Thanks.

Victor: Get well soon.

B PAIRS **Practice the conversation.**

C PAIRS **Practice the conversation again. Use new words.**

A: I have _____.
                  ★
B: I'm sorry to hear that. You should _____.
                                          ★★
A: OK. Thanks.

B: Get well soon.

> **Pronunciation Note**
>
> ◀)) **Listen and repeat.**
> **Which words are**
> **stressed?**
> *I'm **sorry** to **hear** that.*
> *Get **well soon.***

WHAT ABOUT YOU?

PAIRS **Ask and answer:**

If you can't come to class, what do you do?

If you can't go to work, what do you do?

If you can't go to an appointment, what do you do?

> If you can't come to class, what do you do?

> I email my teacher.

A SHOPPPING AT THE PHARMACY

A ◀))) **Listen and point. Listen and repeat.**

1. shampoo **2.** soap **3.** deodorant **4.** toilet paper **5.** toothpaste

B ◀))) **Listen and circle.**

1. Aisle 1 Aisle 2 Aisle 3   **4.** Aisle 1 Aisle 2 Aisle 3

2. Aisle 1 Aisle 2 Aisle 3   **5.** Aisle 1 Aisle 2 Aisle 3

3. Aisle 1 Aisle 2 Aisle 3   **6.** Aisle 1 Aisle 2 Aisle 3

C ◀))) **Listen and repeat.**

A: Excuse me. Where's the deodorant?

B: In Aisle 3.

A: I'm sorry. Where?

B: Aisle 3.

D **PAIRS Look at the picture. Practice the conversation.**

A: Excuse me. Where's the ____?

B: In Aisle ____.

> **Speaking Note**
>
> To ask someone to repeat, you can say: *I'm sorry. Where?*

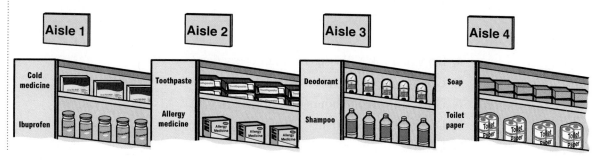

WHAT ABOUT YOU?

GROUPS Ask 3 classmates: What do you buy at the pharmacy?

What do you buy at the pharmacy?

I buy toothpaste and medicine.

A long and healthy life

GET READY

Are you healthy?

READ

◀)) **Skim the article. How many tips are in the article? Listen and read the article.**

HOW TO HAVE A HEALTHY LIFE

Dr. Smith's
Health Page

Be Happy
Think about the good things in your life.

Be Friendly
Visit your friends and family often.

Exercise
Exercise for 2.5 hours every week. Don't sit for a long time. Stand up and walk around a little bit every hour.

Learn New Things
Study English. Visit the library. Learn new sports.

Sleep
Sleep 7–8 hours every night. Take a short nap in the day.

Eat and Drink Well
Eat fruits, vegetables, and fish. Don't eat too much. Drink 8 glasses of water every day.

CHECK YOUR UNDERSTANDING

Now take Dr. Smith's health quiz. Check [✓] Yes or No.

	Yes	No
1. Do you think about the good things in your life?	☐	☐
2. Do you eat fruit every day?	☐	☐
3. Do you eat vegetables every day?	☐	☐
4. Do you drink 8 glasses of water every day?	☐	☐
5. Do you take naps?	☐	☐
6. Do you sleep 7–8 hours every night?	☐	☐
7. Do you study English?	☐	☐
8. Do you visit friends often?	☐	☐
9. Do you visit family often?	☐	☐
10. Do you exercise every week?	☐	☐

How healthy are you?
6–10 *Yes* answers = You're very healthy.
0–5 *Yes* answers = Read Dr. Smith's advice again!

WRITING

Write about your remedies

STUDY THE MODEL

Read Min's home remedies.

> I have many home remedies.   For a stomachache, I drink tea.
> For a cough, I take a hot shower.   For a sore throat, I eat honey.
> For a headache, I lie down.   For a cold, I drink water and rest.

CHECK YOUR UNDERSTANDING

Write Min's home remedies.

Problem	Min's Remedy
a cough	
a headache	
a stomachache	
a sore throat	
a cold	

BEFORE YOU WRITE

Complete the chart with your home remedies.

Problem	My Remedy
a cough	
a headache	
a stomachache	
a sore throat	
a cold	

WRITE

**Write about your home remedies. Look at the model and your chart.
Then copy the sentences on a separate piece of paper.**

For a cough, I _____.

For a headache, I _____.

For a stomachache, I _____.

For a sore throat, I _____.

For a cold, I _____.

GRAMMAR

See page 151 for your Grammar Review.

VOCABULARY See page 158 for the Unit 7 Vocabulary.

Find the word that is different.

1. teaspoon	appointment	tablet	tablespoon
2. runny nose	sore throat	fever	stomach
3. leg	eye	nose	mouth
4. twice a day	lie down	breathe in	sit on the table
5. toothpaste	soap	cough	shampoo
6. deodorant	hot shower	chicken soup	tea
7. rest	sleep	exercise	take a nap

SPELLING See page 158 for the Unit 7 Vocabulary.

CLASS Choose 10 words for a spelling test.

LISTENING PLUS

A **CLASS** Watch each video.
Write the story of Min's day on a separate piece of paper.

Min doesn't feel well.

B **PAIRS** Choose one of these conversations.
Role play the conversation for the class.

Talk about common ailments. (See page 91.)

Make an appointment. (See page 96.)

Ask for items in a store. (See page 99.)

NOW I CAN

PAIRS See page 89 for the Unit 7 Goals. Check ☑ the things you can do.
Underline the things you want to study more. Tell your partner.

> I can ____. I need more practice with ____.

8 Ana's New Home

MY GOALS

Learn About:

☐ The home

☐ Rooms

☐ Furniture

☐ Housing questions

☐ Workplaces

☐ Transportation

☐ Bus signs

☐ Traffic signs

Go to MyEnglishLab for more practice after each lesson.

Ana Sánchez

Ana   *Today*

I'm excited! I'm going to move to a new apartment.

103

Describe your home

HOUSING

A ◀))) **Listen and point. Listen and repeat.**

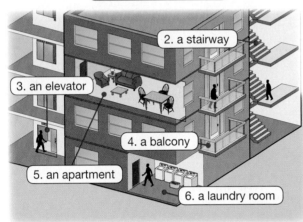

1. an apartment building
2. a stairway
3. an elevator
4. a balcony
5. an apartment
6. a laundry room

7. a house
8. a yard
9. a window
10. a garage
11. a door
12. a driveway

B ◀))) **Listen. For each conversation, circle 2.**

1. elevator
yard
laundry room

2. windows
driveway
balcony

3. garage
yard
driveway

4. stairway
laundry room
balcony

WHAT ABOUT YOU?

PAIRS Check [✓] the things in your home. Then describe your home.

☐ an elevator
☐ a stairway
☐ a balcony
☐ a laundry room

☐ a garage
☐ a yard
☐ a driveway

> I live in an apartment. It has a balcony.

> Sounds nice!

Speaking Note

To respond positively, you can say:
Sounds nice!
Nice!
It sounds great.

GET READY TO WATCH

Ana is telling Victor about an apartment.
Guess. Why?

WATCH

A ◼◀ **Watch the video.**
Was your guess correct?

B ◼◀ **Watch the video again. Circle the word. Write the word.**

1. Tina is Ana's _____.
<u>sister / friend</u>

2. Tina has a new _____.
<u>house / apartment</u>

3. The apartment has two _____.
<u>bedrooms / bathrooms</u>

4. Ana wants to _____ with Tina.
<u>live / work</u>

C ◼◀ **Watch the video again. Circle the answer.**

Victor asks, "What's the apartment like?" He means, "____"

a. I like the apartment.

b. Tell me about the apartment.

c. It's a nice apartment.

CONVERSATION

A ◀ൢ **Listen and read. Listen and repeat.**

Victor: What's the apartment like?

Ana: There are two bedrooms. And there's a big living room.

B **PAIRS** **Practice the conversation.**

C **PAIRS** **Practice the conversation again. Talk about different rooms.**

A: What's the apartment like?

B: There are two _____s. And there's a big _____.
★   ★★

WHAT ABOUT YOU?

PAIRS **Think about your home. Ask and answer:** What is your favorite room?

What is your favorite room?

My favorite room is the kitchen.

There is/there are

○○○○○○ **STUDY**

There is	There are
There is a bedroom.	**There are** two bedrooms.
There is a bathroom.	**There are** two bathrooms.

Grammar Note

There is = There's

○○○○○○ **PRACTICE**

A Write *There is* or *There are*.

1. _There are_ six apartments in the building.

2. _____ a laundry room.

3. _____ three bedrooms.

4. _____ two stairways.

5. _____ an elevator.

6. _____ a garage.

B 🔊 **Listen and check your answers.**

C Look at the picture.
Write sentences about
the apartment.
Use *There is* or *There are*.

1. _There is a living room._

2. _____

3. _____

4. _____

5. _____

6. _____

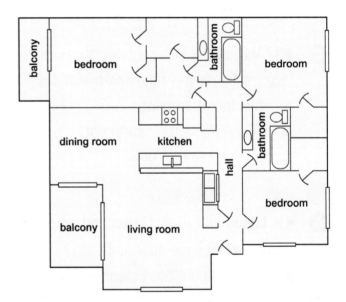

PUT IT TOGETHER

PAIRS **Ask and answer:** What is your home like?

What is your home like?

Well, there are two bedrooms.
There's one bathroom.

Speaking Note

When you are thinking about what
to say, you can say: *Well, . . .*

106 UNIT 8

PRACTICAL SKILLS

Furniture

FURNITURE

A 🔊 **Listen and point. Listen and repeat.**

1. a lamp
2. a bed
3. a dresser
4. a desk

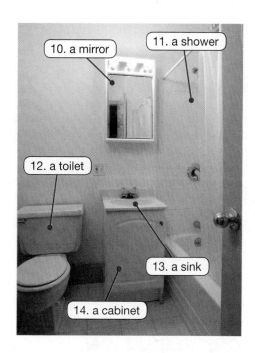

10. a mirror
11. a shower
12. a toilet
13. a sink
14. a cabinet

5. a bookcase
6. a sofa
7. a chair
8. a table
9. a rug

B 🔊 **Listen. For each conversation, circle 2.**

1. cabinets
   sinks
   table

2. sofas
   lamp
   rug

3. table
   chairs
   rug

4. dresser
   desk
   bed

C **What is in your home? Complete the chart.**

Bedroom	Kitchen	Bathroom
bed	sink	toilet

WHAT ABOUT YOU?

PAIRS **Ask and answer:** What's in your kitchen? What's in your living room?

What's in your kitchen?

There's a refrigerator.

What else?

Speaking Note

To continue the conversation, you can say: *What else?*

5

Answer questions about housing

 GET READY TO WATCH

Victor asks Ana questions about the
apartment. Guess. What does he ask?

WATCH

A ◼◀ **Watch the video.**
Was your guess correct?

B ◼◀ **Watch the video again. Circle Yes or No.**

1.	The apartment is on Washington Street.	Yes	No
2.	The rent is $500 a month.	Yes	No
3.	The apartment has new appliances.	Yes	No
4.	The apartment has a laundry room.	Yes	No
5.	The building has a garage.	Yes	No

C ◼◀ **Watch the video again. Answer the question.**

Does Victor know Tina? _____

CONVERSATION

A ◀)) **Listen and read. Listen and repeat.**

Victor: Is there a security guard?

Ana: Yes, there is.

Victor: Is there an elevator?

Ana: Yes, there is.

B **PAIRS Practice the conversation.**

C **PAIRS Practice the conversation again. Use different words.**

A: Is there a _____?
              ★
B: Yes, there is.

A: Is there a _____?
              ★
B: Yes, there is.

Pronunciation Note

Use rising intonation for
yes/no questions.

◀)) **Listen and repeat.**

Is there a security guard?↗

Is there an elevator?↗

WHAT DO YOU THINK?

◼◀ **PAIRS** Watch the video again. Is it a good apartment? Explain your answer.

Is it a good apartment?

Yes. I think . . .

Is there/are there

STUDY *Is there/are there*

Questions	Answers	
Is there a garage?	Yes, **there is**.	No, **there isn't**.
Are there appliances?	Yes, **there are**.	No, **there aren't**.

PRACTICE

A Write *Is there* or *Are there*.

1. _____Is there_____ a laundry room?
2. _____ appliances in the apartment?
3. _____ beds in the bedrooms?
4. _____ a desk in the bedroom?
5. _____ chairs in the dining room?
6. _____ a lamp in the living room?

B ◀)) **Listen and check your answers.**

C **Write.**

1. **A:** Is there a balcony?
   B: Yes, ___there is___ .

2. **A:** Are there a lot of windows?
   B: Yes, _____ .

3. **A:** Are there two bathrooms?
   B: No, _____ .

4. **A:** Is there a yard?
   B: No, _____ .

5. **A:** Are there closets?
   B: No, _____ .

6. **A:** Is there an elevator?
   B: Yes, _____ .

D ◀)) **Listen and check your answers.**

PUT IT TOGETHER

PAIRS Ask and answer questions about the picture.

Is there a bed?

No, there isn't.

a bed	a shower	chairs	cabinets
a lamp	a sink	a rug	bookcases
a mirror	a sofa	a table	windows

GET READY TO WATCH

Victor is meeting Tina for the first time.
What do you say when you meet someone for the first time?

WATCH

A ■◀ **Watch the video.**
Check [✓] the questions Victor asks Tina.

☐ What's your name? ☐ Where do you work?

☐ Where do you live now? ☐ Why do you need a roommate?

B ■◀ **Watch the video again. Circle the answer.**

1. What does Tina call Victor?

    a. Victor **b.** Mr. Sánchez

2. What does Victor call Tina?

    a. Tina **b.** Ms. Wells

CONVERSATION

A ◀))) **Listen and read. Listen and repeat.**

Victor: Where do you work?

Tina: I work in an office. I'm an office assistant.

B PAIRS **Practice the conversation.**

C PAIRS **Practice the conversation again. Use different workplaces and occupations.**

A: Where do you work?

B: I work in a _____. I'm a _____.
               ★   ★★

WHAT ABOUT YOU?

GROUPS Have more conversations about where you work.
Copy and complete the chart.

Where do you work?

I work in a restaurant.

What do you do?

I'm a cook.

Name	Workplace	Occupation

GET READY TO WATCH

Marie has a long trip to work.

How long is your trip to work?

 WATCH

A ▐◀ **Watch the video. Circle the answer.**

1. Where is Ana's new apartment?

    a. Close to work.   **b.** Far from work.

2. Marie's bus ride is _____.

    a. long   **b.** short

3. What does Marie do on the way to work?

    a. She reads.   **b.** She sleeps.

B ▐◀ **Watch the video again. Circle the answer.**

Marie says, "It's nice!" She's talking about _____.

a. Ana's new apartment   **b.** Marie's bus ride   **c.** Ana's phone

CONVERSATION

A ◀)) **Listen and read. Listen and repeat.**

Ana: How do you get to work?

Marie: I take the bus.

B **PAIRS** Practice the conversation.

C **PAIRS** Practice the conversation again. Talk about different forms of transportation.

A: How do you get to work?

B: I _____.
      ★

ROLE PLAY

PAIRS Ask questions about transportation.

How do you get to school?

I walk.

Place	Transportation
school	
work	
the post office	
the supermarket	

PRACTICAL SKILLS

Bus signs

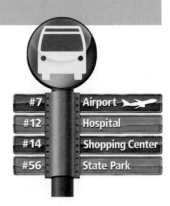

 THE BUS STOP

A **Read the sign. Answer the questions.**

1.	Which bus goes to the state park?	Bus # _____.
2.	Which bus goes to the airport?	Bus # _____.
3.	Which bus goes to the hospital?	Bus # _____.
4.	Which bus goes to the shopping center?	Bus # _____.

#7	Airport
#12	Hospital
#14	Shopping Center
#56	State Park

B ◀⎺))) **Listen and repeat.**

A: Excuse me. Which bus goes to the shopping center?

B: Bus number 14.

A: Thank you.

Speaking Note

To ask someone a question, you can start with: *Excuse me.*

C **PAIRS** **Student A:** Cover Student B's information. Ask about the buses.
Student B: Cover Student A's information. Ask about the buses.

Excuse me. Which bus goes to the library?

Bus number 15.

Thank you.

Student A	
Library	15
School	#16
Police station	
Airport	#17
Hospital	
Train station	#60
Post office	

Student B	
Library	#15
School	
Police station	#18
Airport	
Hospital	#80
Train station	
Post office	#90

WHAT ABOUT YOU?

PAIRS **Ask and answer:** Do you take the bus? Where do you go?

Do you take the bus?

Yes. I take the number 17.

Where do you go?

To work.

PRACTICAL SKILLS

Traffic signs

 TRAFFIC SIGNS

A ◀))) **Listen and point. Listen and repeat.**

1. _____ 2. _____ 3. _____ 4. _____

5. _____ 6. _____ 7. _____ 8. _____

B **Write the words under the signs in Exercise A.**

No Left Turn	No Parking	Stop
No U Turn	One Way	Don't Walk
Train Crossing	Walk	

C ◀))) **Listen and check your answers.**

D ◀))) **Listen. Circle a or b.**

1. (a.) STOP   b.   5. a.   b. STOP

2. a.   b.   6. a.   b.

3. a.   b.   7. a.   b.

4. a.   b.   8. a.   b.

WHAT ABOUT YOU?

GROUPS What other traffic signs do you see? Draw a sign you see. Show it your group. What does it mean?

> This sign means . . .

A good neighborhood

GET READY

Do you like your neighborhood?

READ

◀)) **Listen and read the article. As you listen, mark the pauses in the text.**

Mr. Parker

I like my neighborhood./The houses are big./All the houses have garages and big yards.

The streets are quiet. There are not a lot of cars. There are no buses or trucks.

We are far from the train station and airport. Our neighbors are quiet, too.

There are good schools in my neighborhood. It's a good neighborhood.

Ms. Tate

I like my neighborhood. My neighborhood is fun. There are restaurants on our street. There's a park close to our apartment. There's a library two blocks away.

My neighborhood is convenient. There is a bus stop across from my apartment. I take the bus to work. I walk to the supermarket and the pharmacy. They are very close to my apartment.

My neighborhood is friendly. I talk to my neighbors every day. It's a good neighborhood.

CHECK YOUR UNDERSTANDING

A **What is in each neighborhood? Complete the chart.**

| a bus stop | ~~big yards~~ | good schools | quiet neighbors |
| apartments | friendly neighbors | houses | stores |

Mr. Parker's Neighborhood	Ms. Tate's Neighborhood
big yards	

B **PAIRS** Do Mr. Parker and Ms. Tate live in the same neighborhood? Explain your answer.

12 Write about your home

STUDY THE MODEL

Read the description.

This is my home. There are two bedrooms. There is one balcony. There is a big living room. There is a small kitchen. There are two sofas in the living room. There is a big table in the living room. There are two chairs in the kitchen. There are four windows in the living room.

CHECK YOUR UNDERSTANDING

Look at the floor plan.
Read the model again.
There is 1 mistake in the model.
Circle the mistake.

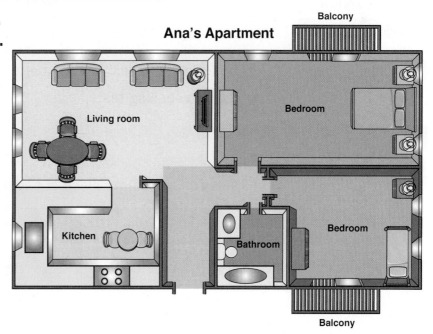

Ana's Apartment

Balcony

Living room

Bedroom

Kitchen

Bathroom

Bedroom

Balcony

BEFORE YOU WRITE

Think about your home. Draw a floor plan of your home.

WRITE

Write about your home. Look at the model and your floor plan.
Then copy the sentences on a separate piece of paper.

This is a floor plan of my home.

There is _____.

There is _____.

There are _____.

There are _____.

There is _____.

There is _____.

There are _____.

There are _____.

GRAMMAR

See page 152 for your Grammar Review.

VOCABULARY   See page 158 for the Unit 8 Vocabulary.

Find the word that is different.

1. mechanic   desk   cashier   security guard
2. garage   bus   train   subway
3. one way   no parking   take the train   no left turn
4. yard   dresser   cabinet   bookcase
5. toilet   shower   stairway   sink
6. mirror   kitchen   living room   hall
7. window   balcony   door   hotel
8. ride   drive   closet   walk

SPELLING   See page 158 for the Unit 8 Vocabulary.

CLASS   Choose 10 words for a spelling test.

LISTENING PLUS

 CLASS   Watch each video.
Write the story of Ana's day on a separate piece of paper.

Ana wants to move. _____

B   PAIRS   Choose one of these conversations.
Role play the conversation for the class.

Talk about rooms. (See page 105.)

Answer questions about housing. (See page 108.)

Talk about transportation. (See page 111.)

NOW I CAN

PAIRS   See page 103 for the Unit 8 Goals.   Check ☑ the things you can do.
Underline the things you want to study more. Tell your partner.

> I can _____. I need more practice with _____.

9 Luka Helps Out

MY GOALS

Learn About:

☐ The weather

☐ Apologizing for being late

☐ Offering to help

☐ Preparing for emergencies

☐ Calling 911

☐ Signs in a hospital

☐ Leaving a voicemail message

☐ Activities

Go to MyEnglishLab for more practice after each lesson.

Luka Petrov

Luka *Today*
I care about my coworkers. I'm always ready to help.

PRACTICAL SKILLS

Talk about the weather

 WEATHER

A ◀)) **Listen and point. Listen and repeat.**

1. It's sunny.

2. It's cloudy.

3. It's windy.

4. It's raining.

5. It's snowing.

B ◀)) **Listen and write.**

cloudy	raining	~~snowing~~	windy	sunny
~~cold~~	cool	hot	warm	cold

1. It's _____cold_____ and _____snowing_____.

2. It's _____ and _____.

3. It's _____ and _____.

4. It's _____ and _____.

5. It's _____ and _____.

C ◀)) **Listen and read. Listen and repeat.**

A: How's the weather today?

B: It's warm and sunny.

PUT IT TOGETHER

PAIRS Ask and answer: How's the weather today?

How's the weather today?

It's hot and windy.

LISTENING AND SPEAKING

Apologize for being late

 GET READY TO WATCH

Luka is late for work.
Are you ever late for work or school? Why?

 WATCH

A **Watch the video. Circle *Yes* or *No*.**

1. Victor is late.	Yes	No
2. Luka is at work.	Yes	No
3. Luka's bus is late.	Yes	No
4. The restaurant is busy.	Yes	No

B ◼◀ **Watch the video again. Circle the answer.**

Why does Luka say, "I'm sorry"?

a. Because he is late.   **b.** Because it is raining.

 CONVERSATION

A ◀))) **Listen and read. Listen and repeat.**

Luka: I'm sorry I'm late.

Victor: What's happening?

Luka: I'm waiting at the bus stop. My bus is late.

Victor: That's OK.

B **PAIRS Practice the conversation.**

C **PAIRS Practice the conversation again. Use different forms of transportation.**

B: I'm sorry I'm late.

A: What's happening?

B: I'm waiting at the _____. My _____ is late.
                                    ★   ★★

A: That's OK.

WHAT ABOUT YOU?

PAIRS Ask and answer: What do you do when you are late ____?

> What do you do when you are late for work?

> I call my manager.

for work
for school
for an appointment
to meet a friend

3 Present continuous

STUDY Present continuous

Affirmative	Negative
I **am** help**ing**.	I **am not** help**ing**.
You **are** help**ing**.	You **are not** help**ing**.
She **is** help**ing**.	She **is not** help**ing**.
Victor **is** help**ing**.	Victor **is not** help**ing**.
We **are** help**ing**.	We **are not** help**ing**.
They **are** help**ing**.	They **are not** help**ing**.
It **is** rain**ing**.	It **is not** rain**ing**.

Grammar Note

| drive | → driving | sit | → sitting |
| take | → taking | put | → putting |

PRACTICE

A **Write.** (are not   is not   are   is)

1. Dan _____ standing.

He _____ sitting.

2. They _____ walking.

They _____ taking the bus.

B ◄))) **Listen and check your answers.**

C **Write. Use the present continuous.**

1. I _____*am studying*_____ English.
          study

2. He _____ a letter.
          read

3. They _____ about
          talk
the weather.

4. You _____ me.
          help

5. We _____ in class.
          sit

6. She _____ to work.
          drive

D ◄))) **Listen and check your answers.**

PUT IT TOGETHER

PAIRS **Tell your partner:** What's happening in your class right now?

Tom is reading.

We are talking.

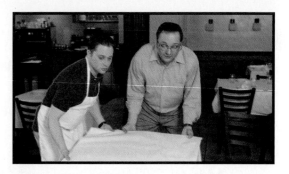

 GET READY TO WATCH

Victor and Luka are moving furniture.
Guess. Why?

 WATCH

Ⓐ ◼◀ **Watch the video.**
Was your guess correct?

Ⓑ ◼◀ **Watch the video again. Circle *Yes* or *No*.**

1.	Victor is helping Luka.	Yes	No
2.	Luka is helping Victor.	Yes	No
3.	Luka and Victor move a table.	Yes	No
4.	A small group is coming for lunch.	Yes	No
5.	Victor is feeling sick.	Yes	No
6.	Luka knows what's wrong with Victor.	Yes	No
7.	Victor lies down.	Yes	No

 CONVERSATION

Ⓐ ◀))) **Listen and read. Listen and repeat.**

Luka: What are you doing?

Victor: I'm moving furniture.

Luka: Can I help?

Victor: Sure. Thanks!

> **Speaking Note**
> To say *no*, say:
> *No, thanks. I'm all set.*

Ⓑ **PAIRS Practice the conversation.**

Ⓒ **PAIRS Practice the conversation again. Talk about different activities.**

A: What are you doing?

B: I'm _____.
       ★

A: Can I help?

B: Sure. Thanks!

WHAT DO YOU THINK?

PAIRS Ask and answer:
What is wrong with Victor?

What is wrong with Victor?

I think . . .

EMERGENCY PLAN

A **Read the emergency information. Who uses the information?**

EMERGENCY INFORMATION

Emergency number: 911
Name of business: _Lakeside Café_
Address: _5305 North Clark Street, Chicago, IL 60640_
Phone: _(773) 555-9918_
Emergency Meeting Place: _Santo Pharmacy on Second Street_

B **Answer the questions.**

1. What is the emergency number? _____

2. What is the restaurant phone number? _____

3. Where is the emergency meeting place? _____

EMERGENCY CONTACTS

A **Read. Complete the sentence.**

Emergency Contacts

Employee Name	Contact Name	Relationship	Phone
Victor Sánchez	_Elma Sánchez_	_wife_	_312-555-3501_

In an emergency call Victor's _____ _wife_ _____. Her name is _____.
Her phone number is _____.

B **Write your emergency contact information.**

Emergency Contacts

Employee Name	Contact Name	Relationship	Phone
_____	_____	_____	_____

WHAT DO YOU THINK?

GROUPS Who is a good emergency contact?
Check [✓] one. Talk with your group.

Who is a good
emergency contact?

I think . . .

☐ a person with a cell phone   ☐ a person in your city   ☐ a friend

☐ a family member   ☐ a person in your home country

LISTENING AND SPEAKING

Call 911

GET READY TO WATCH

Victor is having a heart attack.
Luka calls 911.

What are other 911 emergencies?

WATCH

■◀ **Watch the video.**
Check [✓] the questions you hear.

☐ What's your emergency?   ☐ What's your occupation?

☐ Where are you from?   ☐ What is happening right now?

☐ What's the address?   ☐ What's your phone number?

☐ What's your name?

CONVERSATION

Ⓐ ◀)) **Listen and read. Listen and repeat.**

911: What's your emergency?

Luka: My boss is having a heart attack.

911: What's the address?

Luka: 5305 North Clark Street.

911: 5305 North Clark Street?

Luka: Yes.

> **Speaking Note**
>
> To make sure you understand,
> you can repeat information.
>
> ◀)) **Listen and repeat.**
> **A:** What's the address?
> **B:** 5305 North Clark Street.
> **A:** 5305 North Clark Street?
> **B:** Yes.

Ⓑ **PAIRS Practice the conversation.**

Ⓒ **PAIRS Practice the conversation again.**
Use different emergencies and your own address.

A: 911. What's your emergency?

B: _____.
         ★

A: What's the address?

B: _____.

WHAT DO YOU THINK?

GROUPS Luka calls 911 from his cell phone.
What other ways can you contact 911?

by landline phone?   by computer?

by pay phone?   by texting?

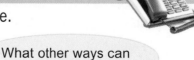

What other ways can
you contact 911?

By . . .

Signs in a hospital

 HOSPITAL

A ◀)) **Listen and point. Listen and repeat.**

1. emergency room

2. waiting room

3. registration

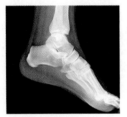

4. radiology and X-rays

5. cafeteria

B ◀)) **Read the directory. Listen to the conversations. Write the floor.**

REGISTRATION	FLOOR 1
EMERGENCY ROOM	FLOOR 1
RADIOLOGY	FLOOR 2
WAITING ROOM	FLOOR 3
CAFETERIA	FLOOR 4

1. _1_

2. ___

3. ___

4. ___

5. ___

C **Match.**

1. I think my hand is broken.

2. My father is having a heart attack.

3. You need to fill out some forms.

4. We are waiting to see the doctor.

5. She is hungry.

a. emergency room

b. radiology and x-rays

c. waiting room

d. registration

e. cafeteria

PUT IT TOGETHER

PAIRS Ask and answer more questions about the hospital in Exercise B.

Where is Registration?

It's on the first floor.

PRACTICAL SKILLS

Leave a voicemail message

VOICEMAIL MESSAGES

A ◀))) **Listen and read. Listen and repeat.**

A: This is the voicemail of Elma Sánchez.
Please leave a message.

B: Hello. This is Nancy Smith from the
emergency room at City Hospital.
Please call me back at (312) 555-2023.
Thank you.

B ◀))) **Listen and write.**

Message 1 (from   for)

1. The message is _____ Bill.
2. The message is _____ Maya.

Message 2 (from   for)

1. The message is _____ Sandi.
2. The message is _____ Joe.

C **PAIRS** **Practice the conversation. Leave more messages.**

A: This is the voicemail of _____.

Please leave a message.

B: Hello. This is _____.

Please call me back at _____.

Thank you.

WHAT ABOUT YOU?

PAIRS **Ask and answer:** How do you leave messages for
your teacher? For your friends? For your manager?

by voicemail
by text message
by email

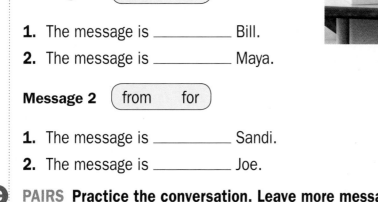

How do you leave messages
for your teacher?

By voicemail.

LISTENING AND SPEAKING

Ask about people's activites

GET READY TO WATCH

Why is Luka answering the phone?
Guess. Where is Ana?

WATCH

A ▪◀ Watch the video. Was your guess correct?

B ▪◀ Watch the video again. Match.

1. What is Victor doing?   **a.** She's cooking.

2. What is Luka doing?   **b.** She's serving customers.

3. What is Min doing?   **c.** He's helping in the dining room.

4. What is Marie doing?   **d.** He's sleeping.

C Circle the answer.

1. Where is Ana?   **a.** at the hospital   **b.** at home

2. Where is Victor?   **a.** at the hospital   **b.** at home

3. Where is Marie?   **a.** in the kitchen   **b.** in the dining room

4. Where is Min?   **a.** in the kitchen   **b.** in the dining room

CONVERSATION

A ◀))) Listen and read. Listen and repeat.

Ana: Are you washing the dishes?

Luka: No, I'm not. I'm helping in the dining room.

B PAIRS Practice the conversation.

C PAIRS Practice the conversation again. Use different activities.

A: Are you _____?
          ★

B: No, I'm not. I'm _____.
                    ★

WHAT DO YOU THINK?

PAIRS Is Luka doing a good job?
Explain your answer.

Is Luka doing a good job?

I think . . .

STUDY Present continuous: *Yes/no* questions

Are you **cooking**?	Yes, I **am**.	No, I'**m not**.
Is she **cooking**?	Yes, she **is**.	No, she'**s not**.
Is he **cooking**?	Yes, he **is**.	No, he'**s not**.
Is Min **cooking**?	Yes, she **is**.	No, she'**s not**.
Are you and Luka **cooking**?	Yes, we **are**.	No, we'**re not**.
Are they **cooking**?	Yes, they **are**.	No, they'**re not**.

Grammar Note

She **is** cooking.

Is she cooking?

PRACTICE

A ◼◀ **Watch the video again. Match.**

1. Is Min cooking?
2. Is Luka washing the dishes?
3. Are Marie and Luka working?
4. Is Marie answering the phone?
5. Are Ana and Victor working?

a. Yes, they are.
b. No, he's not.
c. Yes, she is.
d. No, she's not.
e. No, they're not.

B **Write questions. Use the present continuous.**

1. __Is__ it __raining__?
   _{rain}

2. _____ you _____?
   _{work}

3. _____ she _____?
   _{wash dishes}

4. _____ he _____?
   _{study}

5. _____ they _____?
   _{help}

6. _____ Min and Marie _____?
   _{sleep}

C ◀))) **Listen and check your answers.**

PUT IT TOGETHER

PAIRS Point to a picture. Ask and answer questions about the picture.

Is she sleeping?

No she's not.

1.

2.

3.

GET READY

Where are the emergency rooms in your community?

READ

◀))) **Read the questions on the website.**
What do you think the answers are? Listen and read.

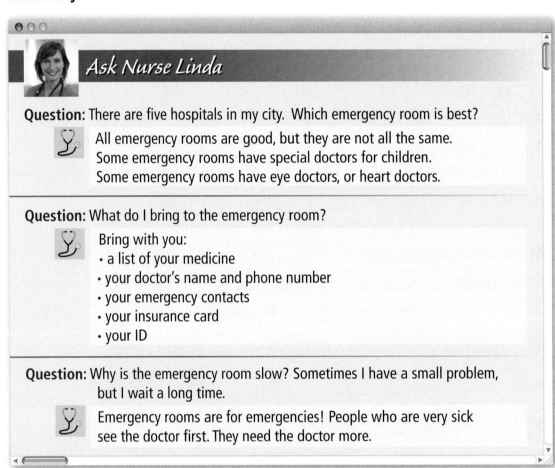

Ask Nurse Linda

Question: There are five hospitals in my city. Which emergency room is best?

All emergency rooms are good, but they are not all the same.
Some emergency rooms have special doctors for children.
Some emergency rooms have eye doctors, or heart doctors.

Question: What do I bring to the emergency room?

Bring with you:
• a list of your medicine
• your doctor's name and phone number
• your emergency contacts
• your insurance card
• your ID

Question: Why is the emergency room slow? Sometimes I have a small problem, but I wait a long time.

Emergency rooms are for emergencies! People who are very sick
see the doctor first. They need the doctor more.

CHECK YOUR UNDERSTANDING

Read again. Circle *Yes* or *No*.

1.	All emergency rooms are the same.	Yes	No
2.	Some emergency rooms have special doctors.	Yes	No
3.	Bring the name of your teacher to the emergency room.	Yes	No
4.	Bring your insurance card to the emergency room.	Yes	No
5.	Emergency rooms are for people with small problems.	Yes	No

Write about your activities

STUDY THE MODEL

Read Victor's online post.

Luka Petrov
to Victor Sánchez

Dear Victor,

I'm glad that you are feeling better. Everything at the restaurant is fine. It's busy!
I'm helping in the dining room.
Min is cooking in the kitchen.
Marie is serving customers in the dining room.
Marie and I are answering the phone.
Get well soon, Victor!

Luka

CHECK YOUR UNDERSTANDING

Answer the questions.

Where is Min? _____

What is Min doing? _____

Where is Marie? _____

What is Marie doing? _____

BEFORE YOU WRITE

Answer the questions. Use your own information.

Where are you? _____

What are you doing? _____

Who is with you? _____

What is he or she doing? _____

WRITE

On a separate piece of paper, write 4 or 5 sentences about what you and your family or friends are doing right now. Look at the model and your answers to the questions.

UNIT 9 REVIEW

GRAMMAR
See page 153 for your Grammar Review.

VOCABULARY See page 159 for the Unit 9 Vocabulary.

Find words for each group. Tell your partner your words.

Activities	Weather	Places
clean the stove	raining	train station

SPELLING See page 159 for the Unit 9 Vocabulary.

CLASS Choose 10 words for a spelling test.

LISTENING PLUS

 CLASS Watch each video. Write the story of Luka's day on a separate piece of paper.

■◀   ■◀   ■◀   ■◀

Luka is late for work.

B **PAIRS Choose one of these conversations.**
Role play the conversation for the class.

Talk about the weather. (See page 118.)

Apologize for being late. (See page 119.)

Offer to help. (See page 121.)

NOW I CAN

PAIRS See page 117 for the Unit 9 Goals. Check ☑ the things you can do.
Underline the things you want to study more. Tell your partner.

> I can _____. I need more practice with _____.

10 Victor's Big Decisions

MY GOALS

Learn About:

- ☐ **Finding a job**
- ☐ **Goals**
- ☐ **Employment ads**
- ☐ **Job applications: Personal information**
- ☐ **Job skills**
- ☐ **Work experience**
- ☐ **Job applications: Employment history**
- ☐ **Congratulating someone**

Go to MyEnglishLab for more practice after each lesson.

Victor Sánchez

Victor *Today*
I love my restaurant, but I need to rest a little bit.

131

PRACTICAL SKILLS

Find a job

WAYS TO FIND OUT ABOUT JOBS

A ◀))) **Listen and point. Listen and repeat.**

1. **look for signs**

2. **look online**

3. **use an employment agency**

4. **look in a newspaper**

5. **talk to friends and family**

B ◀))) **Listen. For each conversation check [✓] 1.**

	1.	2.	3.	4.	5.
Look for signs.					
Look online.	✓				
Use an employment agency.					
Look in a newspaper.					
Talk to friends and family.					

WHAT ABOUT YOU?

GROUPS **Ask and answer:** How do you find out about jobs?

How do you find out about jobs?

I talk to people.

LISTENING AND SPEAKING

2

Talk about goals

GET READY TO WATCH

Victor and Luka are talking about Luka's job. Luka is happy. Guess. Why?

WATCH

A ▣◀ **Watch the video. Was your guess correct?**

B ▣◀ **Watch the video again. Circle *Yes* or *No*.**

1. The restaurant is quiet these days.	Yes	No
2. Luka is doing a great job.	Yes	No
3. Luka is working in the dining room and the kitchen.	Yes	No
4. Luka has a new job.	Yes	No
5. Victor has a new job.	Yes	No
6. Lakeside Café needs a new server.	Yes	No

C ▣◀ **PAIRS Watch the video again. Answer the questions with a partner.**

1. Does Victor need rest? _____

2. Is Victor happy with Luka's work? _____

3. Why does Victor need a new dishwasher? _____

CONVERSATION

A ◀)) **Listen and read. Listen and repeat.**

Victor: What are your goals for the future?

Luka: I'd like to be a manager.

B **PAIRS Practice the conversation.**

C **PAIRS Practice the conversation again. Talk about different goals.**

A: What are your goals for the future?

B: I'd like to be a _____.
★

WHAT ABOUT YOU?

GROUPS Ask and answer: What are your goals for the future?

What are your goals for the future?

I'd like to be a nurse. What about you?

PRACTICAL SKILLS

Read an employment ad

JOB ADS

A **Read the ads. Are they for the same job or different jobs?**

○○○ www.jobsnet.com

Lakeside Café Lakeside Café is looking for a dishwasher. We are a small family restaurant in a busy neighborhood.

Job Title: Dishwasher
Hours: Full-time: weekdays and weekends
Pay: $11–$13 per hour
Business: Lakeside Café
5305 North Clark Street
Chicago, IL 60640

Click here to print the application.
Please call (773) 555-2943 to make an appointment.

Dishwasher
FT, wkdys & wknds.
$11–$13/hr
Lakeside Café
5305 North Clark Street
Call (773) 555-2943

B **Read the ads again. Circle _Yes_ or _No_.**

1.	The job is for a dishwasher.	Yes	No
2.	It is a part-time job.	Yes	No
3.	The pay is $10 per hour.	Yes	No
4.	You need to make an appointment.	Yes	No

C **Look at the ads in Exercise A. Match.**

1. wknds	**a.** full-time
2. wkdys	**b.** weekdays
3. hr	**c.** part-time
4. FT	**d.** hour
5. PT	**e.** weekends

Language Note

Full-time = 35–40 hours a week
Part-time = 1–34 hours a week

WHAT ABOUT YOU?

GROUPS Which is better for you—part-time or full-time? Why?

Which is better for you—part-time or full-time?

Part-time is better for me. I go to school.

Job application: Personal information

○○○○○ **PERSONAL INFORMATION**

A Read the form. Who is applying for a job?

Name: _____ Pedro _____ Cabral _____
FIRST   MIDDLE   LAST
Address: __ 1855 West 19th Street __ Chicago ___ IL ___ 60608 __
STREET ADDRESS   CITY   STATE   ZIP
Phone: __ (773) 555-5098 ____ Email: __ pcabral23@kmail.com ___

Date available to start: __ 11/3/14 __

Check [✓] days and times available:

	Sun.	Mon.	Tue.	Wed.	Thurs.	Fri.	Sat.
Morning	✓			✓	✓	✓	✓
Afternoon	✓	✓	✓	✓	✓	✓	✓
Evening	✓	✓	✓	✓	✓	✓	✓

B **PAIRS** Ask and answer questions about Pedro.

Is Pedro available on Sunday mornings?   Yes, he is.

C Write your own information.

Name: _____
FIRST   MIDDLE   LAST
Address: _____
STREET ADDRESS   CITY   STATE   ZIP
Phone: _____ Email: _____

Date available to start: _____

Check [✓] days and times available:

	Sun.	Mon.	Tue.	Wed.	Thurs.	Fri.	Sat.
Morning							
Afternoon							
Evening							

WHAT ABOUT YOU?   When are you available to work?

GROUPS Ask and answer:
When are you available to work?

I'm available on Monday mornings and Tuesday afternoons.

5

Talk about job skills

GET READY TO WATCH

Pedro is interviewing for the dishwasher job.
Guess. What questions does Victor ask?

WATCH

A ■◀ **Watch the video.**
Check [✓] Pedro's skills:

☐ operate a dishwasher

☐ drive a truck

☐ lift 40 pounds

☐ ride a bike

☐ fix a dishwasher

☐ speak two languages

☐ cook

B ■◀ **Watch the video again. Answer the question.**

What equipment can Pedro fix? _____

CONVERSATION

A ◀))) **Listen and read. Listen and repeat.**

Pedro: I can operate a restaurant dishwasher.

Victor: Can you lift up to 40 pounds?

Pedro: Yes, I can.

B PAIRS **Practice the conversation.**

C PAIRS **Practice the conversation again. Talk about different skills.**

A: I can _____.
       ★

B: Can you _____?
       ★

A: Yes, I can.

WHAT DO YOU THINK?

GROUPS Does Pedro have good interview skills? What does he do well?

Does Pedro have good interview skills?

I think . . .

GRAMMAR

6 Can/can't

STUDY *Can/can't*

I **can lift** 20 pounds.	I **can't lift** 100 pounds.
You **can lift** 20 pounds.	You **can't lift** 100 pounds.
She **can lift** 20 pounds.	She **can't lift** 100 pounds.
Victor **can lift** 20 pounds.	Victor **can't lift** 100 pounds.
They **can lift** 20 pounds.	They **can't lift** 100 pounds.

> **Grammar Note**
>
> can't = can not = cannot

PRACTICE

A ◀ᴺ))) **Listen. Write ✓ or ✗.**

clean floors	✓
wash windows	✗

1. Sue

make copies	
use a computer	

2. Jim

drive a truck	
drive a car	

3. Scott

speak English	
speak Chinese	

4. Ann

B **Look at Exercise A. Write sentences about each person.**

1. Sue _can clean floors_____.

   She _can't wash windows_____.

2. Jim _____.

   He _____.

3. Scott _____.

   He _____.

4. Ann _____.

   She _____.

> **Pronunciation Note**
>
> *Can* is short. *Can't* is long.
>
> ◀ᴺ))) **Listen and repeat.**
>
> *I can speak English.*
> *I can't speak Arabic.*

C ◀ᴺ))) **Listen and check your answers.**

PUT IT TOGETHER

> I can ride a bike.
> I can't drive a truck.

PAIRS What can you do? Tell your partner about your skills.

drive a truck	speak Spanish	fix things
make copies	use a computer	lift 40 pounds

GRAMMAR

7 Can: Yes/no questions and short answers

 STUDY *Can:* **Yes/no questions and short answers**

Can you **cook**?	Yes, I **can**.	No, I **can't**.
Can Pedro **cook**?	Yes, he **can**.	No, he **can't**.
Can they **cook**?	Yes, they **can**.	No, they **can't**.

Grammar Note

He **can** fix a car.

Can he fix a car?

PRACTICE

A **Look at the chart. Complete the questions and answers.**

1. **A:** _____Can_____ Jack _____cook_____?

   B: Yes, he _____can_____.

2. **A:** _____ Tina _____ a bike?

   B: _____, she _____.

3. **A:** _____ Jack _____ houses?

   B: _____, he _____.

4. **A:** _____ Jack _____ a cash register?

   B: _____, he _____.

5. **A:** _____ Tina _____ two languages?

   B: _____, she _____.

	Jack	Tina
operate a cash register	✓	✗
speak two languages	✓	✗
build houses	✗	✓
ride a bike	✗	✓
cook	✓	✗

B **Read the sentence. Write the question.**

1. They can speak English. _Can they speak English?_____

2. You can fix a sink. _____

3. She can drive a car. _____

4. Sam can use a computer. _____

C ◀))) **Listen and check your answers.**

PUT IT TOGETHER

PAIRS Ask about your partner's skills.

build houses	use a cash register
cook	operate a coffee machine
fix sinks and toilets	ride a bike
lift 40 pounds	speak two languages

Can you build houses?

No, I can't.

LISTENING AND SPEAKING

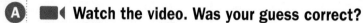

Talk about work experience

8

 GET READY TO WATCH

Look at the picture. Guess.
Does Pedro get the job?

 WATCH

A ◼◀ Watch the video. Was your guess correct?

B ◼◀ Watch the video again. Circle *Yes* or *No*.

1. Pedro wants a part-time job.	Yes	No
2. Victor knows the supervisor at Fast Freddy's.	Yes	No
3. Pedro gets the job at Lakeside Café.	Yes	No
4. Pedro starts work today.	Yes	No

 CONVERSATION

A ◀))) Listen and read. Listen and repeat.

Victor: What was your last job?

Pedro: My last job? I'm still working. I'm a dishwasher at Fast Freddy's.

Victor: Why are you looking for another job?

Pedro: It's a good job, but it's part-time. I need a full-time job.

B PAIRS Practice the conversation.

C PAIRS Practice the conversation again. Talk about different jobs.

A: What was your last job?

B: My last job? I'm still working. I'm a _____ at Fast Freddy's.
★

A: Why are you looking for another job?

B: It's a good job, but it's _____. I need a _____ job.
★★ ★★

WHAT ABOUT YOU?

GROUPS Ask and answer: What was your last job?

What was your last job?

I was a cook.

PRACTICAL SKILLS

Job application: Employment history

WORK EXPERIENCE

A Read Pedro's job application. Which job was first?

Name: *Pedro Cabral*

Work Experience

Employer: *Fast Freddy's*   Job Title: *dishwasher*

Date: *9 / 15 / 12 — present*   Supervisor: *Mike Smith*

Address: *5900 N. Water Street, Chicago*   Phone: *(773) 555-5256*

Employer: *Chima Café*   Job Title: *delivery person*

Date: *3 / 1 / 11 — 8 / 31 / 12*   Supervisor: *Gilmar Costa*

Address: *217 River St., River City*   Phone: *(708) 555-7112*

B Circle the answers.

1. What was Pedro's first job?

   a. a dishwasher   **b.** a delivery person

2. Where was Pedro a delivery person?

   a. at Fast Freddy's   **b.** at Chima Café

3. When was Pedro at Chima Café?

   a. from March 2011 to August 2012   **b.** from May 2012 to October 2014

WHAT ABOUT YOU?

PAIRS Write about your employment history. Tell your partner about your work experience.

Employer: _____

Job Title: _____

Date: from _____ to _____

Supervisor: _____

Address: _____

Phone: _____

What was your last job?

I was a dishwasher.

Where?

At First Street Grill.

LISTENING AND SPEAKING

Congratulate someone

 GET READY TO WATCH

Luka is congratulating Victor.
Guess. Why?

 WATCH

A ◼◀ **Watch the video. Circle the answer.**

1. Why are they having a party?

    a. They got a restaurant award.

    b. They have a new dishwasher.

2. Victor says "Congratulations" to Luka. Why?

    a. Luka graduated.

    b. Luka is now assistant manager.

3. Who does Luka need to meet?

    a. Pedro   **b.** Freddy

B ◼◀ **Watch the video again. Answer the question.**

Why is Victor happy? _____

 CONVERSATION

A ◀ࡍ **Listen and read. Listen and repeat.**

Victor: I have some good news.
        We got the Project Success restaurant award!

Luka: Congratulations!

Victor: Thank you.

> **Speaking Note**
>
> When a person congratulates you, say: *Thank you*.

B **PAIRS Practice the conversation.**

C **PAIRS Practice the conversation again. Talk about different events.**

A: I have some good news. _____!

B: Congratulations!

A: Thank you.

WHAT DO YOU THINK?

GROUPS What are more examples of good news?

What are more examples
of good news?

I think . . .

GET READY

Do you know any volunteers?

READ

◀)) **Listen and read the article. What do you think—why do people volunteer?**

VOLUNTEER Get Work Experience and New Job Skills

Do you want to learn job skills and help people? Become a volunteer!

What do volunteers do?
Volunteers teach. They give rides. They cook and serve food. They answer phones. They make copies. They work in gardens. They fix things. They build houses. Some volunteers even manage businesses!

What do volunteers get?
Volunteers don't get money. They get work experience. They learn new skills. They make new friends. They learn more English.

Where do people volunteer?
People volunteer in many places: schools, libraries, parks, stores, offices, and hospitals.

How do I volunteer?
1. Think about what you like to do.
   Do you like children?
   Do you like gardening?
   Do you like cooking?
   Do you like animals?
   Do you like computers?
2. Ask your school for list of volunteer groups.
3. Start small. Give two hours a week at first.

CHECK YOUR UNDERSTANDING

Write.

1. What do volunteers do?

(answer   give   manage)

They _____ rides.

They _____ phones.

They _____ businesses.

2. What do volunteers get?

(get   learn   make)

They _____ work experience.

They _____ new skills.

They _____ new friends.

12 Write about your goals for the future

 STUDY THE MODEL

Read about Victor's goals.

> **My Goals for the Future**
> I'd like to have two restaurants.
> I'd like to be healthy for many years.
> I'd like to graduate from college.
> I'd like to buy a house.
> I'd like to be a grandfather.

CHECK YOUR UNDERSTANDING

Look at the different kinds of goals. Write Victor's goals in the chart.

Work goals	have two restaurants
Health goals	
School goals	
Housing goals	
Family goals	

 BEFORE YOU WRITE

What are your goals for the future? Complete the chart.

Work goals	
Health goals	
School goals	
Housing goals	
Family goals	

 WRITE

Write about your goals for the future. Use your ideas from the chart.
Then copy the sentences on a separate piece of paper.

I'd like to _____.

I'd like to _____.

I'd like to _____.

I'd like to _____.

I'd like to _____.

GRAMMAR

See page 154 for your Grammar Review.

VOCABULARY See page 159 for the Unit 10 Vocabulary.

Find words for each group. Tell your partner your words.

Job Skills	Occupations	Good News
speak two languages	nurse	I got a job.

SPELLING See page 159 for the Unit 10 Vocabulary.

CLASS Choose 10 words for a spelling test.

LISTENING PLUS

A **CLASS Watch each video.**
Write the story of Victor's day on a separate piece of paper.

Victor talks to Luka about a new job at the restaurant.

B **PAIRS Choose one of these conversations.**
Role play the conversation for the class.

Talk about goals. (See page 133.)

Talk about job skills. (See page 136.)

Congratulate someone. (See page 141.)

NOW I CAN

PAIRS See page 131 for the Unit 10 Goals. Check ☑ the things you can do.
Underline the things you want to study more. Tell your partner.

I can _____. I need more practice with _____.

SUBJECT PRONOUNS

Write. Use the words from the box.

> She   He   ~~They~~   We

1. Ms. Jones and Mr. Cruz are in English class. _____They_____ are classmates.
2. Mr. Lipton is from Brazil. _____ is a teacher.
3. Mrs. Lin is from China. _____ is a student.
4. Mr. Black and I are classmates. _____ are friends, too.

> She   He   They   We

5. Ms. Kim and I are from the U.S. _____ are students.
6. Mrs. Lee is from China. _____ is a manager.
7. Mr. Cruz is from Mexico. _____ is my friend.
8. Mr. and Mrs. Petrov are from Russia. _____ are cooks.

BE: PRESENT TENSE

Look at the chart. Circle the word. Write the word.

Name	Country of Origin	Occupation
Betty	U.S.	teacher
Liz	China	cook
Tom	Russia	cook
Sam	China	teacher

1. My name ____is____ Betty.

is / am

2. I _____ from the United States.

is / am

3. _____ and I _____ teachers.

Sam / Tom   is / are

4. Tom _____ from _____.

is / are   Russia / China

5. _____ and Liz _____ from China.

Tom / Sam   am / are

6. _____ and Tom _____ cooks.

Liz / Sam   is / are

BE: CONTRACTIONS

Write. Use subject pronouns and contractions.

1. Mr. Cruz and Ms. Lee are at school. _They're_ students.

2. Mr. Cueva is not available on Saturdays. _____ available on Sundays.

3. Ms. Chang is at work. _____ a manager.

4. Ms. Sanchez is at school. _____ a teacher.

5. Mr. Sorok is at home. _____ a student.

6. Mr. Rogers and I are here today. _____ off on Monday.

BE: NEGATIVE

Look at the work schedule. Write.

	Sunday	Monday
Ana	✓	✗
Luka	✗	✓
Min	✓	✗
Victor	✓	✗
Marie	✗	✓

1. Ana is at work on Sunday. _She's not_ at work on Monday.

2. Luka and Marie are at work on Monday. _____ at work on Sunday.

3. Victor is at work on Sunday. _____ at work on Monday.

4. Min is at work on Sunday. _____ at work on Monday.

5. Ana and Victor are at work on Sunday. _____ at work on Monday.

POSSESSIVE ADJECTIVES

Circle the word. Write the word.

1. I have a little brother. _____ brother is ten years old.
<small>My / His</small>

2. This is my husband. _____ name is Chuck.
<small>Her / His</small>

3. We have two children. _____ children are 12 and 15 years old.
<small>Their / Our</small>

4. This is my mother. _____ name is Kim.
<small>Her / His</small>

5. My sister has two children. _____ names are Tina and Hannah.
<small>Her / Their</small>

6. You have two children? How old are _____ children?
<small>my / your</small>

BE: YES / NO QUESTIONS

Look at the chart. Write.

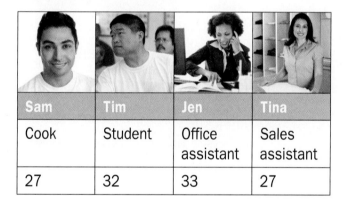

Sam	Tim	Jen	Tina
Cook	Student	Office assistant	Sales assistant
27	32	33	27

1. **A:** _____Is Tim_____ a student?

   B: Yes, he is.

2. **A:** _____ a manager?

   B: No, she's not. She's a sales assistant.

3. **A:** _____ 23 years old?

   B: No, she's not. She's 33 years old.

4. **A:** _____ 27 years old?

   B: Yes, they are.

5. **A:** _____ a teacher?

   B: No. He's a student.

HOW MUCH

Look at the chart. Write the questions.

T-shirt	$8.99
Sweater	$35.00
Jacket	$40.00
Shorts	$15.99
Socks	$5.00
Sneakers	$55

1. **A:** _How much are the socks_ ?

   B: The socks are $_____.

2. **A:** _____ ?

   B: The sweater is $_____.

3. **A:** _____ ?

   B: The shorts are $_____.

4. **A:** _____ ?

   B: The T-shirt is $_____.

5. **A:** _____ ?

   B: The sneakers are $_____.

6. **A:** _____ ?

   B: The jacket is $_____.

QUESTIONS WITH *WHERE*

Write the questions.

1. **A:** _Where are you_ ?
   B: We're at school.

2. **A:** _____ ?
   B: She's at work

3. **A:** _____ ?
   B: He's at home.

4. **A:** _____ ?
   B: They're at the hospital

5. **A:** _____ ?
   B: I'm in the kitchen.

6. **A:** _____ ?
   B: I'm at the store.

UNIT 5 **GRAMMAR REVIEW**

THE IMPERATIVE

Write. Use the words from the box.

~~Call~~	close	go	Put
Save	Turn	Turn off	write

1. _____Call_____ the repairman. Don't call the manager.

2. _____ right! Don't turn left.

3. Don't turn on the power. _____ the power.

4. _____ the food on the stove. Don't put it in the refrigerator.

5. _____ money at the supermarket. Use coupons.

6. Don't _____ a check. Use a money order.

7. Turn left! Don't _____ straight.

8. Open the door. Don't _____ it.

PREPOSITIONS OF LOCATION

Look at the map. Match.

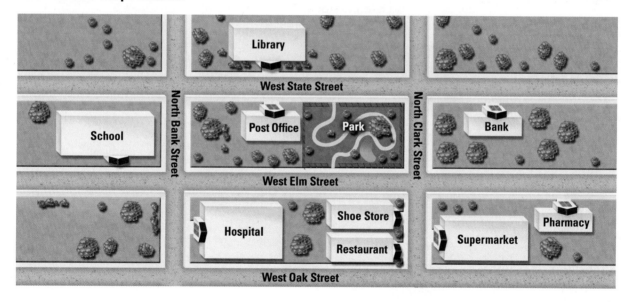

1. Excuse me. Where's the library?
2. Where is the school?
3. Excuse me. Where's the restaurant?
4. Where is the supermarket?
5. Where is the post office?

  a. It's across from the library.
  b. It's next to the shoe store.
  c. It's across from the post office.
  d. It's on West Elm Street.
  e. It's across from the restaurant.

GRAMMAR REVIEW

SIMPLE PRESENT TENSE

A **Write.**

1. We _____*have*_____ apples and oranges. We _____ apples or oranges.

    <u>have</u> <u>not need</u>

2. We _____ bananas. We _____ bananas.

    <u>not have</u> <u>need</u>

3. The soup _____ carrots. She _____ carrots.

    <u>have</u> <u>not like</u>

4. She _____ the soup. She _____ the salad.

    <u>not want</u> <u>want</u>

5. They _____ a carton of eggs. They _____ more cereal.

    <u>need</u> <u>not need</u>

B **Look at the pictures. Write the correct form of *like*.**

I like potatoes.
I don't like onions.

I like potatoes.
I don't like mushrooms.

I like onions.
I don't like mushrooms.

1. Marie _____*likes*_____ potatoes.

2. Marie _____ onions.

3. Victor and Marie _____ potatoes.

4. Victor and Min _____ mushrooms.

5. Min _____ onions.

6. Min _____ mushrooms.

SIMPLE PRESENT TENSE: *YES / NO* QUESTIONS

Write. Use the correct form of the verb.

1. **have** **A:** _____Do_____ you _____have_____ a sore throat?

   B: No, I _____don't_____. I _____have_____ a cough.

2. **need** **A:** _____ they _____ more medicine?

   B: Yes, they _____. They _____ more cold medicine.

3. **want** **A:** _____ he _____ tea?

   B: No, he _____. He _____ orange juice.

4. **have** **A:** _____ she _____ a runny nose?

   B: Yes, she _____. She _____ a cold.

5. **need** **A:** _____ I _____ an appointment?

   B: Yes, you _____. You _____ an appointment to see the doctor.

6. **want** **A:** _____ you _____ more allergy medicine?

   B: No, I _____. I _____ some antacid.

7. **have** **A:** _____ you _____ an appointment?

   B: Yes, I _____. I _____ an appointment at 4:30.

8. **need** **A:** _____ we _____ more shampoo?

   B: No, we _____. We _____ soap and toilet paper.

DEMONSTRATIVES

Circle the word. Write the word.

1. **A:** _____This_____ medicine is expensive.
   _{This / These}

   B: Yes, it is. But _____ tablets are on sale.
   _{that / those}

2. **A:** I like _____ shampoo.
   _{that / those}

   B: I don't. I like _____ shampoo.
   _{this / these}

3. **A:** Do you want _____ tablets?
   _{this / these}

   B: No. I want _____ tablets.
   _{that / those}

THERE IS / THERE ARE

Write *is* or *are*.

I have a new apartment! There ___is___ a living room.
1.

There _____ two bedrooms. There _____ a small
2.   3.

kitchen. There _____ new appliances. There _____
4.   5.

windows in every room. There _____ two balconies. There _____
6.   7.

four closets. And there _____ an elevator in the building! It's great!
8.

IS THERE / ARE THERE

Write *is*, *isn't*, *are*, or *aren't*.

1. **A:** ___Is___ there a sofa?

   B: Yes, there ___is___.

2. **A:** _____ there chairs in the living room?

   B: Yes, there _____.

3. **A:** _____ there a rug in the hall?

   B: No, there _____.

4. **A:** _____ there cabinets in the kitchen?

   B: Yes, there _____.

5. **A:** _____ there beds?

   B: No, there _____.

6. **A:** _____ there a table in the kitchen?

   B: No, there _____.

7. **A:** _____ there a sink in the laundry room?

   B: Yes, there _____.

8. **A:** _____ there lamps in the living room?

   B: No, there _____.

PRESENT CONTINUOUS

Look at the pictures. Write.

1. _She's washing_ the dishes.

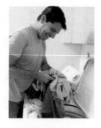

2. _____ laundry.

3. _____ customers.

4. _____ dinner.

5. _____ supplies.

6. _____ the garbage.

PRESENT CONTINUOUS: *YES / NO* QUESTIONS

Write. Use the present continuous of the verb.

1. help **A:** _Are_ they _helping_ ?

B: Yes, they _____.

2. rain **A:** _____ it _____?

B: Yes it _____.

3. clean **A:** _____ he _____ the stove?

B: No, he _____.

4. take out **A:** _____ you and Jim _____ the garbage?

B: Yes, we _____.

5. cook **A:** _____ you _____ dinner tonight?

B: No, I _____.

CAN / CAN'T

Read the skills in the chart. Write.

speak two languages	✓
check supplies	✓
make copies	✗
use a computer	✗

1. A: What are your job skills?

    B: I _____ _____ two languages.

2. A: _____ you _____ supplies?

    B: Yes, I _____.

3. A: _____ you _____ a computer
to make online orders?

    B: No, I _____, but I can learn.

lift up to 50 pounds	✓
ride a bike	✓
drive a car	✗
speak English	✓

4. A: What are his job skills?

    B: He _____ _____ English.

5. A: Good. _____ he _____
up to 50 pounds?

    B: Yes, he _____.

6. A: _____ he _____ a car?

    B: No, _____ _____, but

         he _____ _____ a bike.

serve customers	✓
operate a coffee machine	✓
use a cash register	✓
cook	✗

7. A: What are their job skills?

    B: Well, they _____ _____ customers.

8. A: _____ they _____?

    B: No, they _____.

        But they _____ _____ a coffee
machine.

9. A: _____ they _____ a cash register?

    B: Yes, they _____.

WORD LIST

WELCOME UNIT

a blackboard
a book
a chair
class
close
a desk

listen
look
name
a notebook
open
paper

a pen
a pencil
point
read
repeat
room

school
a table
teacher's name
a whiteboard
write

UNIT 1

Lesson 1
Hello
Hi
shake hands
smile

Lesson 2
first name
last name
middle name

Lesson 3
Excuse me.

Lesson 4
Brazil
China

Haiti
Korea
Mexico
Russia
Somalia
The United States
country
Excuse me?
Where

Lesson 6
a driver's license
a passport
a Social Security card
a student ID

Lesson 7
area code
cell phone
home phone
phone number

Lesson 8
occupations
a cook
a dishwasher
a manager
an office assistant
a sales assistant
a server
a student
a teacher

Lesson 10
Miss
Mr.
Mrs.
Ms.
email address
employer
signature

Lesson 11
a computer
a store
an employment kiosk
fill out an application

UNIT 2

Lesson 1
schedule
days of the week
Monday
Tuesday
Wednesday
Thursday
Friday
Saturday
Sunday

Lesson 3
available
day
home
night

school
weekdays
weekend
work

Lesson 6
a clock
a watch

Lesson 7
an appointment
a break
a class
a meeting
sleep
wake up

Lesson 8
A.M.
P.M.
morning
afternoon
evening
night

Lesson 9
business hours
call
closed
look online
open
a sign
store hours

Lesson 10
early
on time
late

Lesson 11
a flashcard
play back
record
review
study

WORD LIST

UNIT 3

Lesson 2
brother
children
daughter
father
granddaughter
grandfather
grandmother
grandparents
grandson
husband
mother
parents
sister
son
wife

Lesson 3
a baby
a boy
a girl

Lesson 5
a hospital
excited
fine
great
happy
hungry
sad
tired
worried

Lesson 7
January
February
March
April
May
June
July
August
September
October
November
December

Lesson 9
date of birth

Lesson 10
a birthday
a birthday cake
a customer
sing

Lesson 11
a bank
adults
children
coworkers
personal information

UNIT 4

Lesson 1
an apron
a blouse
a coat
a dress
a jacket
a sale
a shirt
a skirt
a sweater
a uniform

Lesson 2
a penny
a nickel
a dime
a quarter

Lesson 3
one dollar
five dollars
ten dollars
twenty dollars

50% off
free
price

Lesson 4
cheap
expensive
pants
shoes
socks

Lesson 6
small
medium
large
extra large
black
blue
brown
gray
green
orange
purple

red
white
yellow

Lesson 7
color
cost
item number
online order
quantity
size
total
website

Lesson 8
break room
dining room
kitchen
office
restroom
storage room

Lesson 10
too big
too long
too short
too small

Lesson 11
a belt
a dress code
a suit
a tie
a T-shirt
jeans
sandals
shorts
sneakers

Lesson 12
wear

WORD LIST

UNIT 5

Lesson 1
appliances
a dishwasher
a dryer
a microwave
a refrigerator
a repair service
a stove
a washing machine

Lesson 3
safety signs
Do Not Enter
Emergency Exit
Fire Extinguisher
No Smoking
Out of Order
Wet Floor

Lesson 4
a bill
electricity

gas
Internet
phone
rent
water
100 one hundred
150 one hundred fifty
200 two hundred
1,000 one thousand
1,150 one thousand,
    one hundred fifty

Lesson 5
a check

Lesson 6
address
apartment (Apt.)
avenue (Ave.)
boulevard (Blvd.)
city
drive (Dr.)

road (Rd.)
state
street (St.)
zip code

Lesson 7
a bank
a library
a park
a pharmacy
a post office
a supermarket

Lesson 8
across from
next to
on

Lesson 9
an envelope
a money order
a package

a post office box
a stamp

Lesson 10
go straight
one block
turn left
turn right

Lesson 11
a coupon
a name brand
a store brand
food
regular price
sale price
save

UNIT 6

Lesson 1
bread
cheese
chicken
fish
meat
milk
pasta
rice

Lesson 2
apples
bananas
beans
onions
oranges
peppers
potatoes
salad
soup
tomatoes

Lesson 3
have
like
need
want

Lesson 4
a bag of carrots
a bottle of juice
a box of cereal
a can of corn
a carton of eggs
a pound of shrimp

Lesson 5
a drink
a green salad
a salad
a sandwich
coffee
dessert
fruit
iced tea
juice

milk
pie
soda
soup
tea
vegetables

Lesson 6
breakfast
lunch
dinner

Lesson 7
broccoli
celery
cucumbers
green beans
lettuce
mushrooms
peas

Lesson 9
a tip
change

a one
a five
a ten
a twenty
a fifty
a hundred

Lesson 10
cash
a check
a credit card
a debit card
a money order

Lesson 11
a cab driver
a delivery person
a hairdresser
a porter
an airport
a train station
percent

WORD LIST

UNIT 7

Lesson 1
arm
back
ear
eye
finger
foot
hand
head
knee
leg
mouth
neck
nose
stomach

Lesson 2
a cold
a cough
a fever
the flu
a headache

a runny nose
a sore throat
a stomachache
medicine

Lesson 3
an earache

Lesson 4
allergy medicine
antacid
cough medicine
pain medicine

Lesson 5
this
that
these
those

Lesson 6
a tablespoon
a teaspoon

every four hours
tablets
twice a day

Lesson 8
Breathe in.
Breathe out.
Excuse me?
Lie down.
Look straight ahead.
Open your mouth.
Roll up your sleeve.
Sit on the table.
Stand on the scale.
Take off your shoes.

Lesson 9
drink tea
eat chicken soup
go to the doctor
rest
take a hot shower
take medicine

Lesson 10
an aisle
deodorant
shampoo
soap
toilet paper
toothpaste

Lesson 11
exercise
healthy
sports
take a nap

Lesson 12
a remedy

UNIT 8

Lesson 1
an apartment
an apartment building
a balcony
a door
a driveway
an elevator
a garage
a house
a laundry room
a stairway
a window
a yard
sounds nice

Lesson 2
a bathroom
a bedroom
a closet
a dining room
a hall

a kitchen
a living room
move

Lesson 4
a bed
a bookcase
a cabinet
a chair
a desk
a dresser
a lamp
a mirror
a rug
a shower
a sink
a sofa
a table
a toilet

Lesson 5
a security guard
new
old

Lesson 7
a cashier
a convenience store
a garage
a hotel
a housekeeper
a mechanic

Lesson 8
drive
get a ride
ride my bike
take the bus
take the subway
take the train
walk

Lesson 9
a bus stop
a police station
a shopping center

Lesson 10
traffic signs
Don't Walk
No Left Turn
No Parking
No U Turn
One Way
Stop
Train Crossing
Walk

Lesson 11
loud
quiet
trucks

WORD LIST

UNIT 9

Lesson 1
It's cloudy.
It's cold.
It's cool.
It's hot.
It's raining.
It's snowing.
It's sunny.
It's warm.
It's windy.

Lesson 2
a subway
a subway station

a train
a train station

Lesson 4
check supplies
clean the stove
do laundry
fix the lawnmower
take out the garbage
wash the dishes

Lesson 5
an emergency contact

Lesson 6
Someone robbed my
   house.
There was an accident.
There's a fire.

Lesson 7
cafeteria
emergency room
radiology and X-rays
registration
waiting room

Lesson 8
a message
voicemail

Lesson 9
cook
serve customers
study

Lesson 11
a heart
an insurance card
slow

UNIT 10

Lesson 1
look for signs
look in the newspaper
look online
talk to friends and family
use an employment
   agency

Lesson 2
a child care worker
a construction worker
a delivery person
a hairdresser
a supervisor
goals

Lesson 3
an employment ad
full-time
part-time

Lesson 4
morning
afternoon
evening

Lesson 5
build houses
drive a truck
fix equipment
lift up to 40 pounds
make copies

operate a machine
speak two languages
use a cash register

Lesson 6
can
can't

Lesson 9
employer
employment history
job title
supervisor

Lesson 10
a party
congratulations
I am now a citizen.
I bought a house.
I got a job.
I got my driver's license.
I graduated.
I passed my English
   test.

Lesson 11
animals
garden
a ride
volunteer

LETTERS AND NUMBERS

ALPHABET

Aa	Ee	Ii	Mm	Qq	Uu	Yy
Bb	Ff	Jj	Nn	Rr	Vv	Zz
Cc	Gg	Kk	Oo	Ss	Ww	
Dd	Hh	Ll	Pp	Tt	Xx	

CARDINAL NUMBERS

1 one
2 two
3 three
4 four
5 five
6 six
7 seven
8 eight
9 nine
10 ten
11 eleven
12 twelve
13 thirteen
14 fourteen
15 fifteen
16 sixteen
17 seventeen
18 eighteen
19 nineteen
20 twenty
21 twenty-one
22 twenty-two
23 twenty-three
24 twenty-four
25 twenty-five
26 twenty-six
27 twenty-seven
28 twenty-eight
29 twenty-nine
30 thirty
31 thirty-one
32 thirty-two
33 thirty-three
34 thirty-four

35 thirty-five
36 thirty-six
37 thirty-seven
38 thirty-eight
39 thirty-nine
40 forty
41 forty-one
42 forty-two
43 forty-three
44 forty-four
45 forty-five
46 forty-six
47 forty-seven
48 forty-eight
49 forty-nine
50 fifty
51 fifty-one
52 fifty-two
53 fifty-three
54 fifty-four
55 fifty-five
56 fifty-six
57 fifty-seven
58 fifty-eight
59 fifty-nine
60 sixty
61 sixty-one
62 sixty-two
63 sixty-three
64 sixty-four
65 sixty-five
66 sixty-six
67 sixty-seven
68 sixty-eight

69 sixty-nine
70 seventy
71 seventy-one
72 seventy-two
73 seventy-three
74 seventy-four
75 seventy-five
76 seventy-six
77 seventy-seven
78 seventy-eight
79 seventy-nine
80 eighty
81 eighty-one
82 eighty-two
83 eighty-three
84 eighty-four
85 eighty-five
86 eighty-six
87 eighty-seven
88 eighty-eight
89 eighty-nine
90 ninety
91 ninety-one
92 ninety-two
93 ninety-three
94 ninety-four
95 ninety-five
96 ninety-six
97 ninety-seven
98 ninety-eight
99 ninety-nine
100 one hundred

LETTERS AND NUMBERS

ORDINAL NUMBERS

1 first
2 second
3 third
4 fourth
5 fifth
6 sixth
7 seventh
8 eighth
9 ninth
10 tenth
11 eleventh
12 twelfth
13 thirteenth
14 fourteenth
15 fifteenth
16 sixteenth
17 seventeenth
18 eighteenth
19 nineteenth
20 twentieth
21 twenty-first
22 twenty-second
23 twenty-third
24 twenty-fourth
25 twenty-fifth
26 twenty-sixth
27 twenty-seventh
28 twenty-eighth
29 twenty-ninth
30 thirtieth
31 thirty-first
32 thirty-second
33 thirty-third
34 thirty-fourth

35 thirty-fifth
36 thirty-sixth
37 thirty-seventh
38 thirty-eighth
39 thirty-ninth
40 fortieth
41 forty-first
42 forty-second
43 forty-third
44 forty-fourth
45 forty-fifth
46 forty-sixth
47 forty-seventh
48 forty-eighth
49 forty-ninth
50 fiftieth
51 fifty-first
52 fifty-second
53 fifty-third
54 fifty-fourth
55 fifty-fifth
56 fifty-sixth
57 fifty-seventh
58 fifty-eighth
59 fifty-ninth
60 sixtieth
61 sixty-first
62 sixty-second
63 sixty-third
64 sixty-fourth
65 sixty-fifth
66 sixty-sixth
67 sixty-seventh
68 sixty-eighth

69 sixty-ninth
70 seventieth
71 seventy-first
72 seventy-second
73 seventy-third
74 seventy-fourth
75 seventy-fifth
76 seventy-sixth
77 seventy-seventh
78 seventy-eighth
79 seventy-ninth
80 eightieth
81 eighty-first
82 eighty-second
83 eighty-third
84 eighty-fourth
85 eighty-fifth
86 eighty-sixth
87 eighty-seventh
88 eighty-eighth
89 eighty-ninth
90 ninetieth
91 ninety-first
92 ninety-second
93 ninety-third
94 ninety-fourth
95 ninety-fifth
96 ninety-sixth
97 ninety-seventh
98 ninety-eighth
99 ninety-ninth
100 one hundredth

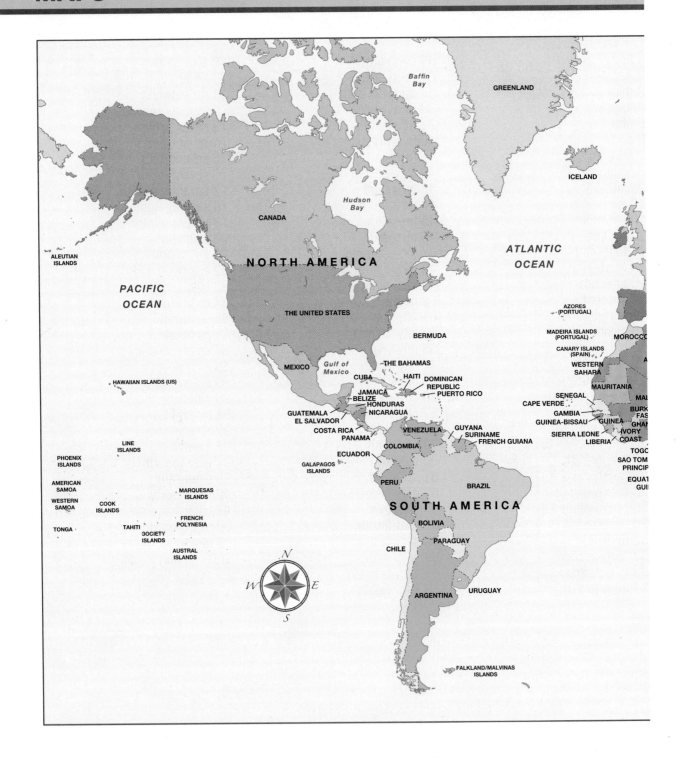

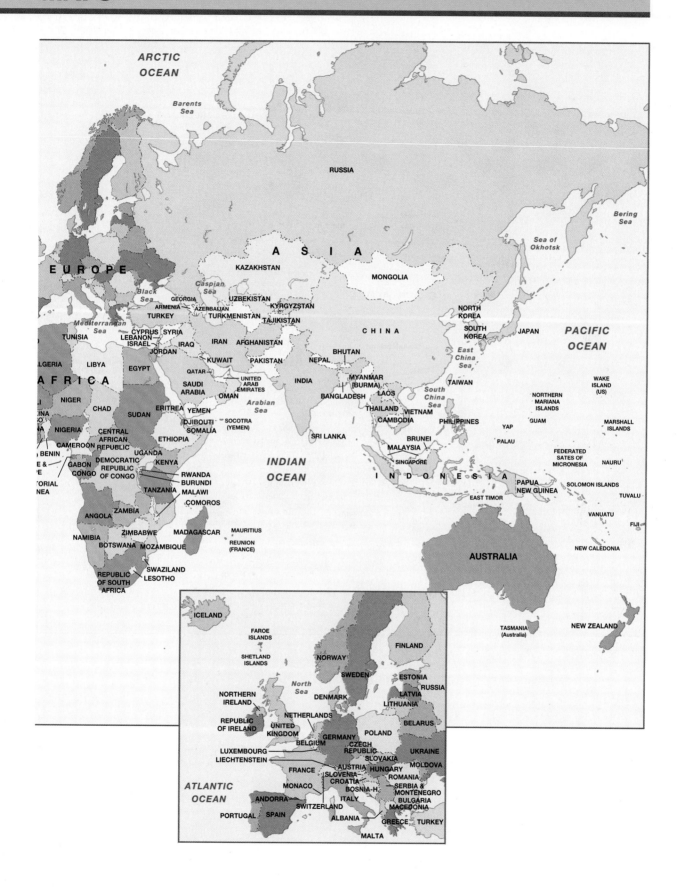

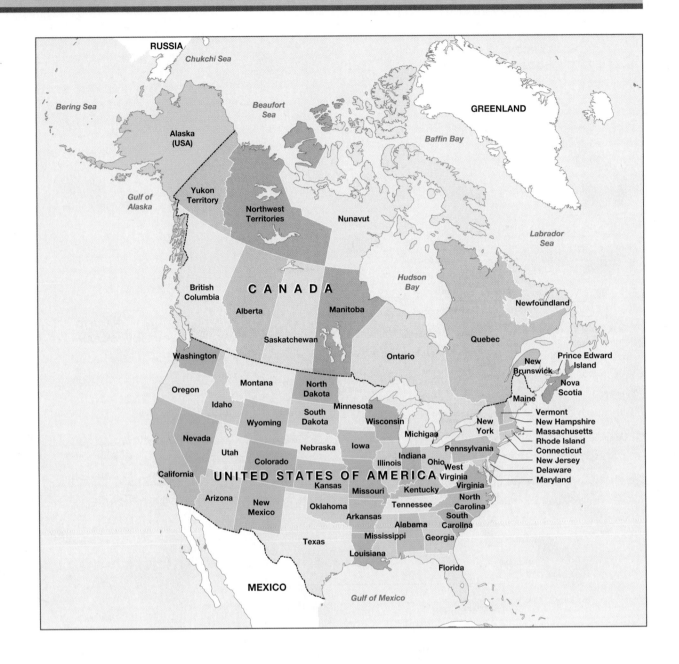

CREDITS

PHOTOS

Cover Photos: Matthew Howe, Photographer. Student book: All original photography by Matthew Howe, Photographer. Page 2 William Perugini/Shutterstock; p. 3 (1) Ljupco Smokovski/Fotolia, (2) Coprid/Fotolia, (3) Datacraft/Getty Images, (4) rottenman/Fotolia, (5) George Dolgikh/Fotolia, (6) Pshenichka/Fotolia, (7) dimedrol68/Fotolia, (8) Altay Kaya/Fotolia, (9) Hoenstine/Fotolia, (10) imageegami/Fotolia; p. 7 Samuel Borges/Fotolia; p. 9 (left) Jason Stitt/Fotolia, (right) pkchai/Fotolia; p. 10 (1) snowwhiteimages/Fotolia, (2) Tyler Olson/Fotolia, (3) Rob/Fotolia, (4) Image Source IS2/Fotolia; p. 12 (1) babimu/Fotolia, (2) jamesh77/Fotolia; p. 14 James H. Pickerell/Fotolia; p. 16 TERRY HARRIS/KRT/Newscom; p. 25 (left) ra2 studio/Fotolia, (middle) Jeffrey Blackler/Alamy, (right) pablo h. caridad/Fotolia; p. 26 (bottom) xalanx/Fotolia; p. 28 (left) Jeffrey Blackler/Alamy, (right) nasir1164/Fotolia; p. 29 (left) George Wada/Fotolia, (right) withGod/Fotolia; p. 30 (top to bottom) MelisendeVector.com/Fotolia, Moneca/Shutterstock, Anna Velichkovsky/Fotolia, RA Studio/Fotolia, Moneca/Shutterstock; p. 35 (2) Blend Images/Glow Images, (3) GlowImages/Alamy, (5) Christopher Meder/Shutterstock, (6) CREATISTA/Shutterstock, (8) Digital Media Pro/Shutterstock, (9) Imagesource/Glow Images, (10) Goodluz/Shutterstock, (12) MBI/Alamy, (14) Purestock/Alamy; p. 36 (left) Suprijono Suharjoto/Fotolia, (right) Dan Kosmayer/Fotolia; p. 37 Blend Images/Alamy; p. 45 (right) szefei wong/Alamy; p. 49 usmint.gov; p. 50 (a) 2happy/Shutterstock, (b) Voronin76/Shutterstock, (c) Garsya/Shutterstock, (d) Steve Stock/Alamy; p. 54 Corbis RF/Alamy; p. 58 (business left & right) Minerva Studio/Shutterstock, (casual left & right) kurhan/Shutterstock, (bus cas left) Minerva Studio/Shutterstock, (bus cas right) Stanislav Komogorov/Shutterstock; p. 59 Shawlin Mohd/Fotolia; p. 64 (a) Santhosh Kumar/Fotolia, (c) tribalium81/Fotolia, (d) Jenny Thompson/Fotolia, (e) Monkey Business/Fotolia, (f) igor/Fotolia; p. 72 Blend Images/Alamy; p. 76 (1) bakerjim/Fotolia, (2) Daddy Cool/Fotolia, (3) Viktor/Fotolia, (4) Bochkarev Photography/Shutterstock, (5) Gregory Gerber/Shutterstock, (6) Adam Gilchrist/Shutterstock, (7) Michaela Stejskalova/Shutterstock, (8) Elenathewise/Fotolia; p. 80 (top left) sarsmis/Shutterstock, (bottom left) pavel siamionov/Fotolia, (top right) monticellllo/Fotolia, (bottom right) MSPhotographic/Fotolia (bottom) karandaev/Fotolia; p. 84 Africa Studio/Fotolia; p. 85 (3) Garsya/Shutterstock; p. 87 (pizza) Sergejs Rahunoks/Fotolia, (fries) ildar akhmerov/Fotolia, (chicken) Maksim Shebeko/Fotolia; p. 90 (top) Maridav/Sutterstock, (bottom) Kurhan/Fotolia; p. 95 (1) Elenathewise/Fotolia, (3) Mario7/Shutterstock; p. 100 Yuri Arcurs/Fotolia; p. 107 (top left) ep stock/Fotolia, (bottom left) roseburn3Dstudio/Shutterstock, (right) BUILT Images/Alamy; p. 109 yampi/Shutterstock; p. 113 (1) dcwcreations/Shutterstock, (2) iQoncept/Fotolia, (3) Paul Brennan/Shutterstock, (4) Carlos Santa Maria/Fotolia, (5) Tom Grundy/Shutterstock, (6) geargodz/Fotolia, (7) Feng Yu/Shutterstock, (8) Darryl Brooks/Shutterstock; p. 114 (top) Corbis Flirt/Alamy, (bottom) Supri Suharjoto/Shutterstock; p. 120 (left) AISPIX by Image Source/Shutterstock, (right) sborisov/Fotolia; p. 121 (left) eddie toro/Fotolia, (right) David Gilder/Fotolia; p. 123 (left) marisha5/Fotolia, (right) Henryk Sadura/Fotolia; p. 124 (1) S. Meltzer/PhotoLink/Getty Images, (2) Elenathewise/Fotolia, (3) 1exposure/Alamy, (4) jovannig/Fotolia, (5) Arcaid Images/Alamy; p. 125 Tetra Images/Alamy; p. 126 (left) Image Source IS2/Fotolia, (right) michaeljung/Fotolia;

CREDITS

p. 127 (1) wavebreakmedia/Shutterstock, (2) CandyBox Images/Shutterstock, (3) Corbis RF/Alamy; p. 128 Rocketclips, Inc./Shutterstock; p. 132 (1) David R. Frazier Photolibrary, Inc./Alamy, (2) Lev Dolgatsjov/Fotolia, (3) wavebreakmedia/Shutterstock, (4) Elenathewise/Fotolia, (5) Ariel Skelley/Getty Images; p. 137 (1) chagin/Fotolia, (2) DragonImages/Fotolia, (3) Sarah Cheriton-Jones/Fotolia, (4) bst2012/Fotolia; p. 142 KidStock/Getty Images; p. 147 (left to right) Tyler Olson/Fotolia, Hill Street Studios/Glow Images, Yuri Arcurs/Alamy, Monkey Business Images/Shutterstock; p. 153 (1) michaeljung/Shutterstock, (2) Monkey Business/Fotolia, (3) auremar/Shutterstock, (4) Dustin Dennis/Fotolia, (5) Jetta Productions/Getty Images, (6) Rob Byron/Shutterstock.

ILLUSTRATIONS

Laurie Conley, p. 97 (8–9); ElectraGraphics, Inc., pp. 14, 44, 63, 106, 162–164; Brian Hughes, pp. 53, 69 (top), 79, 99 (top), 104; Dusan Petricic, pp. 118; Rob Schuster, pp. 50 (bottom), 70, 71, 73, 112, 149; Gary Torrisi, pp. 10, 56, 69 (middle), 97 (1–7); TSI Graphics, pp. 25 (top), 95, 99 (bottom), 115; TSI Graphics/John Kurtz, pp. 83, 90, 94; TSI Graphics/Monika Roe, p. 78; Anna Veltfort, p.3 (top).